MW00356428

RAP *and* REDEMPTION *on* DEATH ROW

RAP AND REDEMPTION ON DEATH ROW

Seeking Justice and Finding Purpose behind Bars

ALIM BRAXTON *and* MARK KATZ

THE UNIVERSITY OF NORTH CAROLINA PRESS *Chapel Hill*

© 2024 Alim Braxton and Mark Katz
All rights reserved

Design by Lindsay Starr
Set in Charis and Industry
by codeMantra

Manufactured in the United States of America

Library of Congress Cataloging-in-Publication Data
Names: Braxton, Alim, author. | Katz, Mark, 1970– author.
Title: Rap and redemption on death row : seeking justice and finding purpose behind bars /
Alim Braxton and Mark Katz.
Description: Chapel Hill : University of North Carolina Press, [2024]
Identifiers: LCCN 2023047517 | ISBN 9781469678702 (cloth ; alk. paper) |
ISBN 9781469678719 (paperback ; alk. paper) | ISBN 9781469678726 (epub) |
ISBN 9798890887344 (pdf)
Subjects: LCSH: Braxton, Alim. | Death row inmates—North Carolina—Raleigh—
Biography. | Rap musicians—North Carolina—Raleigh—Biography. | African American
Muslims—North Carolina—Raleigh—Biography. | BISAC: MUSIC / Ethnomusicology |
BIOGRAPHY & AUTOBIOGRAPHY / Cultural, Ethnic & Regional / African American & Black |
LCGFT: Autobiographies.
Classification: LCC HV8701.B73 A3 2024 | DDC 364.66092 [B]—dc23/eng/20231214
LC record available at https://lccn.loc.gov/2023047517

To my sister Keisha Braxton.
May Allah have mercy on her soul.

CONTENTS

List of Illustrations | ix

Acknowledgments | x

Preface by Mark Katz | xiii

PART I

Dear Mama, I Am a Murderer | 3

Five Letters | 7

Hip Hop Is My Life | 9

Abortion or Adoption | 16

Bigger Lover | 19

Being Biracial | 23

Hymn of H.I.M. (He Is Me) | 26

Jeannie | 28

Marriage in Paris | 34

Alhamdulillah! | 37

One Who Has Knowledge | 39

My Creative Process | 43

It Ain't Just Me | 46

My Raleigh | 49

Descent into Crime | 53

We Had Just Kidnapped a Man | 57

Why Didn't I Just Leave? | 59

Oh My God, What Have I Done? | 62

Meaner, Angrier, Deadlier | 66

Orientation at Caledonia | 69

Convict Carnival | 75

Two Codes | 79

Owning the Canteen | 81

The Bible Don't Say Nothing about Pork | 85

Slave Labor | 89

Ready 4 War | 92

I Need a New Shank | 94

Toxic Masculinity | 97

I Had to Put Steel in Him | 102

Mercy on My Soul | 107

PART II

Welcome to Death Row | 113

Death Row Is No Life of Luxury | 118

Years in Segregation | 120

Islam and Black Nationalism | 122

Allahu Akbar! | 128

Living among the Innocent | 131

Unbreakable | 135

My First Recordings | 138

All about the Money | 141

Total Loss of Privacy | 144

Original Gangster | 146

A Gangster Trying to Be Muslim | 150

Finding a Producer | 153

He Doesn't Deserve to Be Here | 156

One Life | 159

Dreamville and the Nightmare | 163

What's the Point in Trying to Do Good? | 165

Hoops and Obstacles | 167

Why Rappers Should Listen to Country Music | 170

My Baby Sister Keisha | 173

Almost Like She Was in Paradise | 176

Waking Up in a Different Country | 178

White Cop | 182

Welcome Back to Unit One | 185

Due Process? | 189

Celebrating in the Hole | 191

Checking In at Central Prison | 193

Thirty-Seven Days in the Hole (Excerpt) | 196

The Alim Team | 200

Anger Is a Privilege That I Don't Have | 203

The Zoom Solution | 205

A Major Milestone | 209

Jay-Z | 212

The Best Human Being I've Ever Met | 214

It Was a Good Day | 218

ILLUSTRATIONS

Excerpt, letter from Alim Braxton to Mark Katz, August 19, 2019 | xiv

Letter from Alim Braxton to Marie Braxton, December 9, 1997 | 4

Alim Braxton rapping on the prison phone | 14

Marie Braxton | 21

Jeannie Bunch | 33

List of books requested by Alim Braxton | 41

Draft of "It Ain't Just Me" | 45

Braxton family photo | 52

"Murderer Spared the Death Penalty" | 64

Offense and Disciplinary Report, 1994 | 67

Death Row dayroom, Central Prison | 115

Death Row cell, Central Prison | 116

Death chamber viewing room, Central Prison | 117

Alim Braxton and Sabur Tyler | 161

Sabur Tyler | 168

Keisha Braxton | 174

Excerpt, letter from Alim Braxton to Mark Katz, June 22, 2020 | 187

Cover art for "If I'm a Killer" | 210

Jeannie Bunch | 216

ACKNOWLEDGMENTS

Alim Braxton, a.k.a. Rrome Alone

I have to begin by giving all praise to Allah. All credit and glory belong to Him, and it is solely by His grace and mercy that I am not only alive and communicating my thoughts and words in this book but also able to record my rhymes—a dream of mine for over thirty-five years.

Next, I've got to shout out my family who have been by my side and supported me every step of the way. My mom has been my number one supporter and has seen me at my absolute lowest in life. I love you, Ma! Look at what your firstborn has accomplished. I'm so happy that you've had a chance to see me rise from the dirt.

I've got to shout out my brother, Chris, a.k.a. Doc, hands down my day one greatest fan. You've been bigging me up since '86, even memorizing some of my earliest rhymes! You believed in me before the rest of the world ever heard of Rrome Alone. You were nodding to my rhymes in the living room at the crib, and you still rock everything I record like it's on loop!

I've got to shout out my sister, Keisha, who passed away on February 5, 2020. I'm just thankful you got a chance to hear a few of my songs before you left. I miss you so much, and I wish you could be here to see your big bro making his debut; but despite your absence your memory is always alive in my heart. You believed in me so much that you wanted to start a record label! And you laid the foundation for everything I'm doing right now. You built the infrastructure and established AHAD Music Group (AMG) and I'm gonna rep that for life, baby girl!

I also have to shout out my wife, Jeannie Bunch. I love you, baby. I feel so blessed being not only your husband but your favorite rapper as well. You were my motivation to first start recording back in 2018, and you've been there the whole time, listening to my dreams and believing in me and encouraging me and occasionally telling me that I'm the man!

Shout-out to my sister, Dee Dee. Your work ethic and boss attitude have definitely been an inspiration for me, as well as your encouragement to not be like those other rappers: to spit that fire but talk about something good and not glorify the bad. I've tried to use that as a guide, even when I find myself tempted to compete with what everybody else is doing.

I've got to shout out my right-hand man, my *akhi*, my brother, and close friend, Sabur. Yo man, you the only person who has seen and heard everything. You know what nobody else was able to witness. Outside of my family, there ain't nobody that believes in me like you do. You was the only ear that I had, day and night, to pour this dream into, and you believed in it even more than me. I hate the fact that you've had to endure the past thirty years of your life in prison for a crime you didn't commit and that you had to land here on Death Row. Allah is my witness, as long as I have the voice to speak, I'm going to do the best I can to let the world know who you are: that Stacey Tyler, a.k.a. Sabur, is an innocent man on Death Row in North Carolina, and I pray that Allah exonerates you and clears your name for the world to see!

Shout-out to my friend and advocate Tessie Castillo for opening up so many opportunities in the field of public speaking and for really lighting my fire to write. Thanks for being consistent in my life.

Next, I've got to shout out Michael Betts II, my original engineer/audio documentarian and good friend and little brother. Yo man, you helped me tread this path and sacrificed countless hours of your time without pay. I could never have accomplished this without you. You recorded all my vocals when I was just rapping a cappella over the phone. You posted me on SoundCloud. You stuck with me when there was no incentive to do so, and you still make time for me every week despite being a new dad who gets very little sleep! Yo man, I am indebted to you, and I'm grateful to have you as a friend.

I've got to shout out the distinguished professor Mark Katz, my good friend and musical facilitator. Without you, this book wouldn't have been possible. You've opened doors and opportunities for me that I would have never been able to access on my own. You've plugged me in on so many levels, and I've just got to say thank you for taking a chance with me, for responding to my first letter despite the fact that I was on Death Row. Before I met you, I was rapping a cappella, and you helped me get to a whole 'nother level. You are the man, and I'm honored to have you as a friend.

Shout-out to my number one producer, the illest in the game, Nick Neutronz. Yo man, the magic we make in the studio is out of this world. I love working with you, and I appreciate all the time and money you've poured into those phone calls so that we could record this music. We got something special. I can't imagine doing this with anybody else. Thank you for believing in me and for pushing some of your stuff to the background just to make space for me. Above all, I got a friend for life.

Last, I've got to shout out Wordsmith, CEO of NU Revolution Entertainment, for giving me an opportunity to get my music heard on a larger platform. A lot of people didn't believe in me because of my phone-recorded vocals, but you told me from day one that not only did you want to help me because you believed in what I was doing but you wanted to be my friend as well.

I've been blessed to have such good people around me, and I thank you all for believing in me and getting my voice heard. Now it's time to make history!

Mark Katz

The first person I must acknowledge, of course, is Alim Braxton. He is a remarkable man, thinker, writer, and artist and a testament to the human possibility of radical, positive change. I am grateful for our partnership and proud to call him a friend.

Many people have supported this book over the past few years and in such a variety of ways. I hope it will suffice to offer my deepest thanks and attest that this book owes so much to all of them: Frank Baumgartner, Michael Betts II, Stephanie Bouis, Chris Braxton, Marie Braxton, Jeannie Bunch, Megan Busbice, Tessie Castillo, Lucas Church, Alexis Dixon, Gretchen Engel, Jennifer Ho, Cerron T. Hooks, Beth Jakub, Carol Jakub, Anna Katz, Evelyn Katz, Warren Katz, Sarah Lindmark, Nick Low-Beer, Destiny Meadows, Joseph Megel, John Powell, Helen Spielman, Jennifer Thompson, Stacey "Sabur" Tyler, Ken Weiss, and Wordsmith. Thanks, also, to all the students who took my course, Music and Incarceration in the United States, at the University of North Carolina at Chapel Hill and who offered excellent feedback on the book, and to my wonderful Carolina colleagues for their encouragement. Finally, a big thank-you to all the people at UNC Press who made this book possible.

PREFACE

By Mark Katz

MAILED FROM CENTRAL PRISON was printed across the top of the envelope. That was the first thing I noticed when I pulled the letter from my faculty mailbox. I read it as I stood in the green-linoleumed mailroom of the Music Department at the University of North Carolina at Chapel Hill. "Dear Mr. Mark Katz," began the letter dated August 19, 2019. "I am a reformed prisoner, writer, and rapper on North Carolina's Death Row."

The return address gave the writer's name as Michael J. Braxton, but the letter was signed "Alim," and that's how I'll refer to him. People who have known him at different times in his life call him Jerome, Rome, Michael, Mikhail Yeshua Yisraeli, or Big Bank. Alim is his Muslim name, and it is how he now introduces himself.

When Alim first wrote to me, he was facing a technological problem. The problem was a lack of technology. He was a rapper seeking to record an album, but he had no microphone, no music production software, no computer, no studio, no producer. Nothing about being on Death Row is conducive to recording an album, and it is not a place that fosters creativity or hope for the future. As Alim later wrote to me, in a vast understatement, "This isn't exactly the most cheerful place in the world." All Alim had was his voice and the poor-quality prison phone. Remarkably, he had already managed to record a few songs, vocal tracks with no accompanying music, or a cappellas, as they are called. But he wasn't happy with the results. His voice was muffled and distorted, and he couldn't find anyone who could make them sound better. That's why he wrote to me. The previous week he had read an article in the local paper about a hip hop summer program I had created at UNC, and it occurred to him that I might be able to help.

I wasn't sure if I wanted to offer my help. I didn't know him, and after all, this request was coming from a convicted murderer. I held onto the letter for more than a month, unsure of what to do. I decided to write back because I was intrigued by his story and moved by his passion. I also saw an earnestness in his neatly handwritten letter that amplified the sincerity of his words, as when he wrote: "I know my situation may seem despairing and perhaps unlike anyone you've worked with before, but despite the

I know my situation may seem despairing and perhaps unlike anyone you've worked with before, but despite the circumstances I still have faith and I still have a dream, and I believe that with the right sound and someone who knows what to do with my vocals I can accomplish something BIG!

Excerpt, letter from Alim Braxton to Mark Katz,
August 19, 2019.

circumstances I still have faith and I still have a dream, and I believe that with the right sound and someone who knows what to do with my vocals I can accomplish something BIG!" When I responded, I offered to see whether any producers I know would be interested in working with him. His excitement jumped off the page in his next letter. "Yes, PLEASE PLEASE PLEASE connect me with some producers who would be happy to provide some beats for me!!!" I posted a request on Facebook, and Nick Low-Beer, a.k.a. Nick Neutronz, a producer I had worked with in the past, generously offered his services at no charge. Soon after that, Alim suggested I call a friend of his, documentarian Michael Betts II, who had recorded him in the past. It wasn't long before a group of us—Betts, Neutronz, and me, as well as the writer and activist Tessie Castillo and the rapper and record-label owner Wordsmith, became a self-fashioned "Alim Team," working to share Braxton's powerful words and music.

Alim Braxton accepts his guilt. "I'm not innocent" was one of the first things he said to me when I visited him at Central Prison in Raleigh in early 2020. He murdered two men, Emmanuel Oguayo and Donald Bryant, during a robbery spree in February 1993, when he was nineteen years old. In 1996, while serving two life sentences plus 110 years for those murders as well as for armed robbery, he killed fellow inmate Dwayne Maurice Caldwell. It was this crime for which he was sentenced, in 1997, to death. (No execution date has been set as of the publication of this book. There is a de facto moratorium on executions in North Carolina as legal challenges to the death penalty work their way through the courts.) Although the man I know is kind and peace-loving, respected by friends and family for his creativity, faith, wisdom, and his skill in resolving conflict, I do not want to minimize his crimes or ignore his victims. His crimes are indefensible, the pain of his victims and their loved ones incalculable. Those he has harmed owe him nothing. This book is not a plea for forgiveness—if anyone chooses to forgive him, it will be on their terms and for their own sake. Alim does not expect forgiveness in this lifetime; he hopes only that God will forgive him in the next. But Alim does believe that through good works, redemption is possible. Crucial to this ongoing journey is his music, and this explains the title of the book, *Rap and Redemption on Death Row*.

Alim raps about many things—his mother, his wife, God, his hometown of Raleigh, and his experiences in prison. But there is one cause that motivates him more than any other: the plight of those wrongfully incarcerated on Death Row. As he wrote in one of his letters:

> One of my goals, through my music, is to generate attention to the issues of capital punishment and specifically to the fact that there are innocent people on Death Row. Since I've been here, I've seen 35 people executed and 7 people exonerated because they were innocent. That's one-fifth of the total number of people executed. Two of my closest friends here on Death Row are innocent: Stacey Tyler and Elrico Fowler. Both of them have been on Death Row over 20 years and don't have the resources or the voice to generate attention to their cases. So that's why I want to use my talent as an MC.

Alim's path to redemption is ultimately a spiritual one, tied to his faith as a devout Muslim. If he can use his music to help save the lives of his friends, he hopes that, in the process, he will save his soul. He explains it this way: "Allah says in the Qur'an that to kill a person is like killing all of mankind, and to save one life is like saving all of mankind. Inshallah, if I can use my music to literally save a man's life on Death Row, then that's in the ultimate service of Allah. I may not accomplish this, but at least my Lord will know that I spent my time trying to make a difference, and I pray that He will forgive me for the wrong I've done in my life."

Alim has made his motivation for recording his music clear. He was motivated to publish this book for similar reasons. The book offers Alim the opportunity to articulate his thoughts and ideas and to chronicle his life in more detail than he can in his music. As he explained in a March 2021 letter, his desire to put his thoughts down on paper has an urgency that most of us are fortunate not to know:

> Sometimes I need to talk about stuff just to get it outside of myself and preserve it on paper, and it's easier to put it in a letter and send it outside of the prison so I don't have to worry about it being confiscated

and read by the guards or the higher-ups. That's one of the total losses of privacy that is a consequence of imprisonment. You don't have the freedom to safeguard and record your own thoughts.

He explained further in a letter from December 2021:

There's certain shit that I don't have the luxury of saying. I can't write it down and keep it in a little journal because nothing that I possess is free from scrutiny. At any time, everything that I think is mine can be seized, including my body, and searched. They can read what I write. It can be used to punish me. I am not free to think. Some of my thoughts are contraband. They are a threat to order and security.

These are well-founded concerns—for example, in 2000, three albums' worth of his lyrics were confiscated and never returned to him. Alim's need to protect his thoughts helps explain why he has written to me so frequently and in such detail. As he once told me, "You know, in some ways you are like my diary."

My role in the creation of this book has consisted of assembling a narrative out of the collected transcripts of his letters to me as of mid 2022—over 500,000 words, about seven times the number of words in this book. I devoted an equal or greater amount of time to revising and editing. I certainly made many decisions—about the overall structure of the book, and about which stories and details to include and which to omit—though I always did so in consultation with Alim, who had the final say in all matters related to content and prose. He has placed a great deal of trust in me in allowing me to shape his words into this book. I am honored to have earned that trust.

This is Alim's story; it is told in his words and in his voice. Nearly everything following this introduction comes from Alim's letters (most to me, a few to others), with some material pulled from his earlier writings. My prose contributions to the main text mostly consisted of context-setting phrases and brief explanations of terms or names that might be unfamiliar to readers, and Alim reviewed and revised what I wrote. As he often pointed out during the revision process, his letters to me were written for "an audience of one," which required making subsequent changes to render the narrative fully intelligible to a broader audience. A recurring and challenging topic of conversation during the revision process was about what *not* to include, particularly about his crimes. Too much detail risks sensationalizing the crimes and dishonoring the lives of his victims and the memories their loved ones carry. Vagueness or euphemism, on the other hand, can diminish the consequences of those truly terrible acts. Alim has said that he would rather not talk about his crimes at all—the experience is traumatic and "intensely shameful." But he feels that that he must account for and address his crimes. We did our best to strike a balance between saying too much and saying too little; whether we have succeeded will be for each reader to judge.

Two years after Alim first wrote to me, one letter had turned into well over one hundred. They document an eventful period of his life, 2019–21, which saw the tragic death of his sister, a cruel and unwarranted stint in solitary confinement, the nationwide protests in the wake of George Floyd's murder, and the reality of living on Death Row in the shadow of COVID-19. This was also the beginning of Alim's recording career, which entailed developing a method to overcome the technological deprivations of prison life and which yielded dozens of songs as well as an animated music video for "Live on Death Row." His work on a full-length album, *Mercy on My Soul*, continued during this time, and the album is intended to be released with the publication of this book.

It wasn't long into our correspondence that I came to believe that Alim's letters were worth preserving and making public, and that is what spurred me to suggest the possibility of a book. Earlier in my career, I had spent many hours in archives reading correspondence by famous musicians. I would count myself lucky anytime I found a single paragraph of interest out of a batch of letters. That is not the case with Alim's correspondence. Each letter he has sent me is rich in detail, vividly written, and compelling. As I read his letters I kept thinking that he was telling stories that needed to be heard, and not just by me. During my first in-person visit with Alim in December 2019, I mentioned that I was digitally scanning his letters to ensure their preservation, and I suggested that he consider donating his letters to an archive at some point. He nodded in response but otherwise didn't react. I had forgotten about the exchange until I received a letter from him the next week. "A couple of things . . . from our conversation really stood out in my mind," he wrote. "The first was your saying that you look at my letters as documents and are preserving them. That you even photo-scan them into a file so they aren't lost. For little old me, the mere thought of that was HUGE! . . . I may have shown some sense of indifference at the moment, but that was only reflexive, . . . an attempt to avoid speechlessness. So yeah, that's like a big deal." In fact, since then, Alim, his mother, Marie Braxton, and I have agreed to donate hundreds of his letters (written to me and to his family, spanning a period of more than thirty years) to UNC's Southern Historical Collection, an important repository of primary sources that documents the culture and history of the U.S. South. It will be the august archive's first collection of materials from an incarcerated person.

So yeah, preserving Alim's letters is a big deal. As he explained, he sees himself as part of a larger history of suppressed Black voices:

> I got to thinking about it more and thought about the value of things like slave narratives. That is a part of history that isn't very well preserved. Sure, we have the official history of slavery, and this includes documents on the exact number of slaves that arrived on which ship and even some of their country of origin. But when it comes to hearing from the slave himself, very little is documented. So when we do discover a particular document written by an actual slave it is valuable because this is a part of history that no one else can tell.

The idea that his letters might be historical documents catalyzed something in Alim: "So I thought, since you are preserving my letters, I may as well chronicle my experiences."

I certainly encouraged him in this. My letters to Alim always included questions about his life, his opinions, his values. In one of my first letters, I wrote, "Because I am a scholar, I love to learn, and I've learned a lot from your letters already. May I continue to ask you questions?" Here are some of the questions I asked him in ensuing letters, which he readily and generously answered: What does hip hop mean to you? Does your faith connect with or influence your identity as an MC, has it shaped your rhymes? What did gangsta rap mean to you when you were younger? What do you mean when you say you are reformed? Do you see music as a way to make peace with your past? How do people listen to music on Death Row? What is Ramadan like at Central Prison? I reciprocated by telling Alim about myself and my work, sending him books, articles, and song lyrics. We read books together and discussed them, including Shane Bauer's *American Prison*, Adam Bradley's *Anthology of Rap*, Miriame Kaba's *We Do This 'Til We Free Us*, Trevor Noah's *Born a Crime*, and Elie Wiesel's *Night*. (I also sent him copies of my books on hip hop, *Groove Music* and *Build*, which he read as attentively as any student I've ever had.) One reason we connected so readily, I believe, was because of our shared intellectual curiosity and love of books. His mother told me that she always thought that if Alim (or Jerome, as she calls him) hadn't gone to prison, he would have become a professor or a lawyer.

Over the course of our correspondence, our shared love of music and curiosity about the world developed into friendship. I distinctly remember the first time he signed one of his letters, "Your friend, Alim." In my response, I wrote, "Thank you for that—it means a lot to me that you think of me as a friend. As we get older, and for men especially, it gets harder to make new friends. It's nice to know it's still possible, even in our not-quite-so-advanced age. So with that, let me sign off as . . . Your friend, Mark." He picked up the thread in his next letter:

> I'm glad you noticed my use of the phrase "your friend" when signing the last letter. I didn't know how you felt about friendship, but I definitely wanted you to know that I had opened up that space in my mind and heart that accessed my friendship, and I wanted you to know that I am your friend. I know that means different things to different people, but for me it's almost kinda playgroundish when I think about it, but I've got your back!

He explained further by referring to an exchange he had with his best friend, Stacey Tyler. Sabur, as Alim calls him, also lives on North Carolina's Death Row.

> Sabur made me realize this a while back. We were talking, and I was trying to inventory my life and recollect some good I had done prior to coming to prison. As unbelievable as it might seem I couldn't recall a single good thing that I had ever done, which naturally had me depressed and feeling like I was an awful person. But Sabur said, "I don't believe that. You are a good dude." I said, "Yeah, maybe now, but I never did anything good on the street." And he said, "I don't think you can find other people out there who see you that way. Look at all the friends you have. Look at your support system. If you were as bad as you think you are, those people wouldn't still be in your life." I had to think about that for a minute, and then I said, "What did I do?" He said, "Most of the time it's the things you do that you're not even aware of. For instance, you make people you are close to feel safe. I know 100% that when I'm with you that I don't have to worry about nobody messing with me." . . . I came out of that conversation feeling good! In a nutshell, I said all that to say that I might not know the qualities that I bring to a friendship, but when I become someone's friend I've got their back. At the very

least, if I'm around you don't have to worry about nobody messing with you! LOL

Friendship is relevant here for two reasons. First, this book is a product of our friendship. This may sound like an odd thing for a scholar to say. We aren't supposed to get emotionally close to our subjects; it is thought to compromise our objectivity. But I couldn't have written this book without Alim's friendship, which required that I have his back, his trust. Everything about my work on this book has blurred lines that, at least traditionally, should remain distinct in my world: the line between scholarship and advocacy, between subjectivity and objectivity, between research consultant and friend, between interviewing and shooting the shit.

Second, friendship is one of the central themes of this book. Alim makes this clear from early on: "Sabur is my best friend. He's my confidant, adviser, and in-house producer. He's heard every rhyme I've got multiple times. He's my number one supporter and biggest fan. I can't give him enough credit. He's just as much a part of this as I am." Alim's path to redemption may be through rap, but Sabur—both as a friend and as a symbol of the many injustices of the U.S. carceral system—is what powers him to follow that path.

Alim's musical and spiritual journey is constantly made more difficult by the everyday reality of life on Death Row. The system is not designed to promote the creative self-expression of incarcerated people. Those who have been in prison for decades, as many of those on Death Row have been, tend to be isolated; they often lose contact with their families or anyone outside the prison walls. They become voiceless and forgotten, mentioned perhaps only when executed. They experience what is known as civil death—an almost complete loss of rights and connection with the world—well before their physical death. Alim recognizes that he is unusual in that his network has grown over the years, and he readily acknowledges that talent and perseverance alone would not have gotten his story the attention it has received. As he explained:

The truth is that the only reason I'm able to do what I'm doing is because I've been blessed with a team. This is really what separates me from others here on Death Row. There are people here that might be more talented than me, but they lack resources. The longer a person is incarcerated, the weaker his support system becomes, and on Death Row we are talking about guys who've been in prison for over 20 years. I want to highlight this fact so people on the outside will realize that there are others in here that are talented, too, and perhaps make resources available to them as has been done for me.

Alim is always quick to recognize the talents of others and to share credit for his successes, whether with friends, family, or God. There is another reason to acknowledge Alim's support system, for it bears witness to the nearly insurmountable obstacles that incarcerated people face when they simply want to make their voices heard.

I'll give one example from Alim's story of how the carceral system works to silence the voices of the incarcerated. In 2020, I started managing the Facebook page that Alim's late sister, Keisha, created to help him communicate with family, friends, and fans. Posts included announcements about new tracks going up on his SoundCloud or YouTube pages, excerpts from his lyrics, and passages from his letters in which he talked about his music or mused on a variety of social and political issues. Many of these posts were designed to seem as if he were speaking directly to his Facebook followers, although they were all repurposed from other sources. At first this approach worked well. The posts received good responses, and Alim always enjoyed reading the comments I copied in my letters to him.

Then, one day in mid-June 2020, I got a frantic text from Alim Team member Michael Betts. We learned that Alim was in solitary confinement, or segregation, as it's called in Central Prison. He had gone for years without any infractions, so the news was a shock. He had lost his phone privileges, so he couldn't immediately tell us what had happened. Several days later I received a letter from him. He reported, with great frustration, that he wasn't told why he was in "the hole." His first thought was that he was being punished for his music and wondered if his song about police violence, "White Cop," might have been the cause.

Weeks passed without word about why he was being disciplined. When he was finally informed of the charges against him, it was for "possessing or using a cell phone or unauthorized recording or communication device." He did not have or use a cell phone, and no such devices were found in his cell. But the prison administration used the Facebook posts—my Facebook posts—as evidence that Alim was violating prison policy.

I immediately wrote to him. "I have to apologize. I'm the reason you are in segregation," I said. I explained how the posts could look like they were coming from inside prison. I also wrote to both the Warden of the Prison and the Commissioner of Prisons for North Carolina, taking responsibility. Along with other members of the Alim Team, I consulted with Alim's lawyer to help him with his appeal. None of this mattered. The infractions remain on his record, and he was stripped of several privileges he had previously enjoyed, including serving as imam, or spiritual leader, to other Muslims on Death Row. One of the most painful aspects of his isolation was his inability to talk with the most important people in his life, his mother, his brother, Chris, and his wife, Jeannie Bunch. Moreover, this episode brought back terrifying memories of the darkest period in his life, when he spent an inhumane stretch of seven-and-a-half years in segregation, from 1996 to 2004.

This was a powerful demonstration of how prisons can, as Alim puts it, "suppress the voices inside." He explained it this way: "Throwing me in the hole is meant to deter me, as well as to deter others. It's also a reminder of who has the power. They're showing me that I don't have to break any rules to be punished. It's a show of force that says, We have the power to crush you if you provoke us." Whether it was intentional or not, this punishment felt like a show of force directed at me as well. To paraphrase Alim, they're showing me that *I* don't have to break any rules *for Alim* to be punished. It forces me to navigate between two unacceptable outcomes: expose Alim to risk by facilitating his freedom of expression or be complicit in the system's suppression of his free speech. I have done both. Writing this book with Alim opens him up to additional punishment. Alim and I have sometimes erred on the side of caution when sharing aspects of his story, whether on social media or in this book, and my worry is that this caution becomes a form of censorship.

This episode taught me a painful lesson: I must accept that in working with Alim, my actions, no matter how well intended and even when I am carrying out his wishes, can do him harm. It is a reminder of the tremendous privileges I have as well as of the consequences of my exercise of those privileges. I am a free white man, a professor with tenure and research funds, and I have tried to deploy those privileges to Alim's benefit. But as I have learned, exercising my privilege can lead to Alim's oppression.

There's no getting around the darkness in this book, which represents the reality of Alim Braxton's life. This book chronicles, often in detail, the crimes he committed and the punishment he has endured. This is not meant to be sensationalistic but to offer instead a first-person perspective that is typically missing from media accounts and court documents. Nothing in this book, however, excuses his crimes or mitigates their severity. Alim's testimony seeks to promote something deeper: understanding. It does so by prompting difficult questions. What leads someone to take another's life? What do we owe those whom we incarcerate? What is, or what should be, the purpose of the United States carceral system? How can the impulses that lead to violence be transformed, and what role can art play in that transformation? Are there limits to redemption?

As much as Alim's story is shot through with darkness, it is also full of joy, hope, and love. We witness in these pages what might seem impossible in such a harsh environment: the unbridled exuberance of the men on Death Row as they excitedly discuss rappers and their rhymes; the enduring power of Sabur's friendship with Alim; the awe Alim feels when he experiences his first video call, seeing his mother in her home for the first time in nearly thirty years; the deep love that develops between Alim and Jeannie Bunch, who married in 2019; the pride and wonderment Alim experiences when he finally hears his music issuing from the prison radio; the steadfast faith that makes his hope for a better future possible. There is no doubt that Alim Braxton is ambitious. He has recorded a full-length album on Death Row. He has written this book. He wants to help free the wrongfully incarcerated. He wants to go home. But at the same time, he wants something simple, something all humans deserve, and which, ultimately, is the goal of this book: "I want it documented that I was here, and that I existed."

RAP *and* **REDEMPTION** *on* **DEATH ROW**

PART I

Dear Mama, I Am a Murderer

ABOUT TWO WEEKS after I was sentenced to die, I wrote a letter to my mother. It was one of my weakest moments. I was broken. A month after I wrote this, a man was executed at Central Prison. He was the last person North Carolina executed in a gas chamber. I saw the COs—correctional officers—celebrating with cupcakes. I saw prisoners getting beaten for protesting. I was traumatized.

Reading this letter again made me cry, remembering where I was at. I was finally coming to grips with the things I had done and who I really was. Peeling away the façade, I recognized that this persona that I had been living had ruined my life and wounded my soul. I had not yet developed true faith in Allah, but this is a young man I can have compassion for. This is a hard one for me to read.

In the Name of Allah the Benificent the Mercyful.
Dear Mama,

How are you? It was so good to see you today. I've been wanting to see you so bad for the past few weeks but we couldn't visit. There's so much emotion inside. So many things I want to be known but can't find the words to say. I'm really hurting inside Mama. Hurting like never before in my life. Right now I'm so unstable that I can't think coherently. I'm unorganized, and out of order. I even find myself wanting a cigarette, a joint, a drink of wine something, anything to make the pain go away if only for a moment. I never knew I had so many tears, so much emotion. I've cried so much that I feel helpless. For so long I've been like a stone, rock solid, closed away from all emotion, hiding from it, afraid to face it. But for some reason the tears feel good Mama. It lets me know that I am a man, I am a human being, I'm not an animal, but I can feel and I can hurt and I have remorse. God knows I have remorse. Why, why, why I ask myself. I am so sorry for all the pain I've caused. I've hurt so many people. You, Chris, Keisha. But not just my family, I've hurt other people's families, Emmanuel Oguayo, Donald Bryant, Dwayne Caldwell. I never thought, I never even cared. But now that I'm faced with the realities of my own death, and how it affects everyone who cares for me, I can't help but to feel the pain of all of those families I've hurt. I've been so wrong. I've done so much evil, and hurt that its unbearable. What can I say, what can I do. I hate myself so much for all of these cruel and senseless murders.

Letter from Alim Braxton to Marie Braxton,
December 9, 1997.

... I am a murderer. Human lives, taken away for nothing. I often grieve because of the atrocities inflicted upon Blacks by whites, and it causes a rage in me Mama because it was evil. But how better am I to take my own brother's life? How can I point finger's, when I have done the same thing. I'll write later.

Look, I'm gonna go. I'll write later. I love you.

Love Always,

Jerome

[DECEMBER 9, 1997]

In the Name of Allah the Beneficent the Merciful
Dear Mama,

How are you? It was good to see you today. I've been wanting to see you so bad for the past few weeks but we couldn't visit. There's so much emotion inside. So many things I want to be known but can't find the words to say. I'm really hurting inside Mama. Hurting like never before in my life. Right now I'm so unstable that I can't think coherently. I'm unorganized, and out of order. I even find myself wanting a cigarette, a joint, a drink of wine something, anything to make the pain go away if only for a moment. I never knew I had so many tears, so much emotion. I've cried so much that I feel helpless. For so long I've been like a stone, rock solid, closed away from all emotion, hiding from it, afraid to face it. But for some reason the tears feel good Mama. It lets me know that I am a man, I am a human being, I'm not an animal, but I can feel and I can hurt and I can have remorse. God knows I have remorse. Why, why, why I ask myself. I am so sorry for all the pain I've caused. I've hurt so many people. You, Chris, Keisha. But not just my family. I've hurt other people's

5

families, Emmanuel Oguayo, Donald Bryant, Dwayne Caldwell. I never thought, I never even cared. But now that I'm faced with the realities of my own death, and how it affects everyone who cares for me, I can't help but to feel the pain of all those families I've hurt. I've been so wrong. I've done so much evil, and hurt that it's unbearable. What can I say, what can I do. I hate myself so much for all these cruel and senseless murders.

I am a murderer. Human lives, taken away for nothing. I often grieve because of the atrocities inflicted upon Blacks by whites, and it causes a rage in me Mama because it was evil. But how better am I to take away my own brother's life? How can I point fingers when I have done the same thing? I'll write later.

Look, I'm going to go. I'll write later. I love you.

Love Always,
Jerome

Though I still had a long way to go, this letter shows my true soul trying to emerge. I am a murderer, but I am also more than that.

Five Letters

ORE THAN twenty years after I wrote that letter to my mama, I wrote five more letters—to the families of the three people I murdered and to the two people I robbed at gunpoint. I wanted each of them to know that I fully accepted the consequences of what I had done. I apologized for my crimes and accepted responsibility for them.

I sent these letters to my attorney. One was addressed to Susan Indula, a taxi driver from Kenya that I robbed in 1992. Another was addressed to Lindanette Walker, who I robbed a year later. And I sent letters to the family of Emmanuel Oguayo, the convenience store clerk from Nigeria I killed, and the family of Donald Bryant, the man I murdered after kidnapping him and holding him in the trunk of his own car for several hours. I robbed Walker and murdered Oguayo and Bryant all on the same night in 1993. Last, I wrote a letter to the family of Dwayne Caldwell, the man—a friend—I knew as Zakil that I killed at Caledonia State Prison Farm in 1996. Despite my criminal convictions, despite my decades of imprisonment, I had never actually taken responsibility for what I'd done. I'd never directly spoken to them or acknowledged their pain. I never apologized. I owed them that.

Because I am prohibited by law from directly contacting any of the victims or their families, my attorneys had to facilitate any contact. They were unable to find Susan Indula or relatives of Emmanuel Oguayo. They sent the letters to Lindanette Walker and to Donald Bryant's family, and both responded to my lawyers. Out of respect for them I will keep their responses private. As for the letter I wrote to the family of Dwayne Caldwell, my attorneys never mailed it. They strongly advised me against sending it because they feared that what I wrote would harm my appeal. But I don't fear the legal system. I fear Allah. One day I am going to meet Him and be held accountable for my deeds, so I need to repent. Repentance means acknowledging that what I did was wrong, having true remorse in my heart, and resolving never to do such harm again. But my lawyers aren't thinking about the Hereafter. They are thinking about the best strategy for the courtroom, and they argued with me until I agreed to postpone the mailing of that letter. My fear then, as now, is that Dwayne Caldwell's mother will pass away before I get the opportunity to apologize to her.

Though I can never justify my crimes, I believe in the possibility of redemption. But what can I do to work toward that goal? What talent do I have? What ability? The one constant in my life, the one thing I absolutely love doing, is writing rhymes. I've been doing it since I first started rapping in 1986. My life story is pretty much written in rhyme form. But rap is only a tool. My ultimate goal is to make amends for the crimes I have committed and to help innocent people on Death Row win their release, starting with my friends Stacey (Sabur) Tyler and Elrico Fowler. I have been granted the ability to articulate things so that other people can understand them, and this is what I believe I have to offer. I just need a platform to be heard. And that's where the raps—and this book—come in.

Hip Hop Is My Life

YOU CAN CALL ME ALIM. My given name is Michael Jerome Braxton, and growing up, my family and friends called me Jerome, or Rome for short. The North Carolina Department of Correction refers me as #0043529, my offender number. A lot of people on Death Row call me Big Bank or just Bank. My dad calls me Michael because his name is also Jerome. My wife, Jeannie, calls me Michael because she swears this is how I introduced myself when we first met in 1991. My rap name is Rrome Alone. I spell Rrome with a double R because I represent Ruff Raleigh, North Carolina. "Alone" is a nod to my many years of solitude and solitary confinement. After I accepted Islam, I took the name Alim, so nowadays, I always introduce myself as Alim. But I'm all of the above. I wear many hats.

I am a prisoner, a writer, and a rapper on North Carolina's Death Row. I've been incarcerated since 1993, when I was nineteen years old, and rap has been and continues to be my vehicle for recording my thoughts, my feelings, and my experiences. Writing rhymes has always been a form of therapy for me. In prison, you are stripped of all your worldly possessions. Very little belongs to you. But my rhymes are mine, and I carry them with me. It's my art that I can plaster on the walls of the shower just for my entertainment. I can spit—that's what we call rapping—to someone or to no one. When the mood strikes and I want to write, it's the greatest escape. The joy I feel after crafting a song, nothing can replace. Nobody else might like it. Hell, nobody else might even hear it, but it's mine and it is *dope*. Besides, it's one of the few things that I can do now that I used to do on the other side of the wall.

Hip hop is my life. KRS-One said: I am Hip Hop. I feel the same way because hip hop has shaped my life and marked so many of my memories. I remember breakdancing in 1983, when I was ten. Back then, I wanted to be a DJ. Rappin' wasn't even a thing yet in my neck of the woods. We had radio stations like 570 WLLE AM (known as Willie) and WKNC 88.1 FM, but they only started playing hip hop gradually. In '83 and '84, we used to go to Sportsworld, a roller-skating rink in Cary. At a certain hour on Sunday nights, they would clear the floor and we would use the rink to breakdance. Some would do windmills, backspins, or headspins, but I was a popper. Back then the illest breakdance songs were electronic songs like "Electric Kingdom" by Twilight 22, "Tour De France" by Kraftwerk, and "Beatbox" by Art of Noise. My mom knew I wanted to be a DJ and bought me a "Welcome Back Kotter" turntable. It was shaped like a lunch box! She bought me that record player and Herbie Hancock's album *Future Shock*, which had the song "Rockit," with all the scratching. That was the first record I ever owned. The first actual rap album that I had was by the Fat Boys. They were my first favorite rappers, but I mainly liked Darren "The Human Beat Box" Robinson. A Fat Boys show was the first and only concert I've ever been to in my life.

I remember my first boombox, my first pair of suede Pumas with the fat laces, my bomber jacket, my parachute pants, my windbreaker, my Kangol, my gold cap for my tooth. I remember writing my first rap in '86, my first battle in '88. Hip hop is the way I talk, my slang, my posture, the way I think. So much of who I am is intertwined with the culture of hip hop. It's in my mind, the thoughts that no one can hear. My language is hip hop. For me, hip hop is also about the preservation and continuance of our culture. I mean Black culture and, by extension, inner-city culture, and the expansion of that culture through deejaying, emceeing, graffiti, and dance.

I started rapping when I was thirteen. I was an eighth-grader at Carnage Middle School in Raleigh. It was my first year at Carnage, as my family had just moved, so I didn't know anyone. I remember in the bathroom one day seeing this kid with a Jheri curl named Larry, and he just started rappin'. It was no more than four or six bars. I think he said, "My name is Larry Love / I'm fly like a dove . . ." After he spit his bars, I asked him what rap was that—I'd never heard it before. He told me that he'd made it up. That just blew my mind. For whatever reason, I thought that only professional rappers like the ones I heard on the radio could rap. I had never thought to even try. But that day I went home and wrote my very first rap—just a few bars—and I memorized it. When I got back to school, I spit it to Larry and a couple of other people in the bathroom and I remember the props everybody gave me. They said it was fresh, it was dope, it was ill. I can't remember many of my old raps anymore, but I do remember the titles of a few. There was "The Alternating Current," "My Drug Rhyme," "Dream Girl," and "Doc the Lover." All of that was between '86 and '88.

On my fifteenth birthday, in 1988, I had a party in my house with about twenty friends. My man Pat Alston was deejaying. He had set up his system: two turntables and a mixer as well as his speakers. We were having a blast and then Pat plugged in his mic and started shouting me out and encouraging me to bust a rhyme. So I went up to the DJ table, got the mic, and Pat threw on the instrumental of a record that was hot at the time, Chubb Rock's "Caught Up." We were just having fun, and Pat recorded it. It was the first time I ever heard my voice recorded to music. I wanted a copy of the tape, but somehow it got lost.

I got kicked out of school that year for calling in a bomb threat as a prank, and after that I dove headfirst into the street. It didn't occur to me to pursue a career as a rapper. I would freestyle off the dome—what we call improvising—but I wasn't putting anything on paper. It was just something I loved to do. One time, though, I heard that Prince Markie Dee from the Fat Boys was sponsoring a rap contest at a Raleigh club called Bentley's. The deadline for entering had been weeks earlier, so I couldn't compete. However, the DJ let me perform anyway. He played the instrumental to Run DMC's "It's Like That" and I *turnt* it out! The crowd went wild. After I did my performance Prince Markie Dee shouted my name out in the club. That was one of my proudest moments.

I was just a teenager then. I'm fifty now, and I've spent most of my life in prison. Hip hop has been my constant companion all this time. Until we were issued electronic tablets in 2022, radio was my only access to music. On Death Row everyone is issued a small AM/FM radio with earphones, and for many years, the best way to hear hip hop was to tune in to WKNC 88.1 FM, a nearby radio station run by NC State University. Every Saturday to Monday, starting around 6 or 7 p.m. they'd play hip hop late into the night. All the hip hop heads in here used to live for 88.1. Even after lock-in (at 10:45 p.m.) you'd hear people banging on the walls to get their neighbor's attention. You'd hear shouts of "eighty-eight-one!" when a good song came on. We loved 88.1 because it was the underground. They played the stuff that we would never hear on commercial radio.

We'd be up till 2 a.m. listening to 88.1 and compare notes the next day. "Yo yo! You hear that Mobb Deep joint?!" "Hell yeah! Man, Prodigy killed that shit!" "Did you hear 'Triumph' by Wu-Tang?" "Who you think had the illest verse?" "Man, I don't know. Inspectah Deck murdered that shit. Nigga said, 'I bomb atomically / Socrates' philosophies and hypotheses / can't define how I be droppin' these mockeries . . . '" "Yo, that was ill, but Raekwon killed that shit, too: 'Ayo, that's amazing, gun in your mouth talk / verbal foul hawk.'" "Yo, what you think he mean when he say, 'verbal foul hawk?'" "I don't know, it might be a play on the words *foul* and *fowl*, like he saying he is verbally foul like he's nasty with the rhymes, or that he's fly like a hawk." "I ain't even think about that shit. Yo, don't sleep on that nigga Cappadonna, though. He said, 'Yo, I twist darts from the heart . . . '" And the conversation might go on for an hour or more with people weighing in about what they thought was dope and what was wack.

I guess with new technology, nobody is listening to radio as much anymore. It's crazy because all those years we had access to music only through our AM/FM radios. We were never allowed to get cassettes, never allowed CDs. When I left the streets in 1993, CDs were still new so I never had any. I had cassette tapes and records. Now MP3s are almost obsolete.

We don't have musical instruments in here. But there are a few dudes who can sing and a few more who can rap. B-Dot raps and sings. His specialty is writing hooks and he has a T-Pain type of vibe. There's 4ever. He's from Brooklyn and is a couple of years older than me. He started back rapping after twenty-five years in prison. He said he was inspired after hearing me spit a verse I wrote. One of the best rappers in here is this guy named Cmurf, who also goes by Twig or El Presidente. Stylistically and content-wise we are so different. When he raps, he likes to pound his chest and snap his fingers. He's ill with beats. I can tell Cmurf to kick the beat from such-and-such song, and he'll hit it right on the spot. He sings a little, too. We chop it up about music all the time. Sometimes we sit at the table and just rap for hours. He'll do one of his songs and I'll do one of mine, back and forth. People come up and listen for a while, and sometimes make requests: "Alim, spit that one about the Prophets," or "Cmurf, do that 'El Presidente.'" Sometimes they compare us. "Cmurf is nice, but Alim be talking about that real shit." Or, "Alim is alright, but did you hear what that nigga Cmurf said?!" As an MC, my biggest influences have been KRS-One, Ice Cube, and Jay-Z. KRS-One is the Teacher, while Ice Cube is the Gangster. My style is a mesh of the two. And Jay-Z— in my opinion, the greatest rapper of all time—inspires me because he represents the ultimate in success as an artist, businessman, and cultural icon.

Out in the dayroom, I'm a human music machine! I kick it with several people and often give them a sample of something I'm working on to see if they're feeling it or not. I might roll up on Jamil and say, "Yo akh, check out this hook and let me know what you think." (Akh is short for *akhi*, "brother" in Arabic.) I'll spit the hook and he might give me some feedback. Sometimes I can get a little participation. I might get Chanton—who raps but prefers reggae—to do a beat for me and Chubb. Or I might tap out a beat, get somebody to do a clap, then ask someone else to hum a melody. And then I'll rap over my human orchestra. But that's rare, because not everybody is musically inclined, and they might get out of sync and grow impatient. Recently, I worked with my producer Nick Neutronz to create an online platform on SoundCloud to showcase other incarcerated artists, and I've even done a few mixtape songs with them. It's called Pen Game Productions. So far Bountry, B-Dot, Cmurf/El Presidente, Messiallah, and Money Ray, all of them on Death Row, have songs on it.

Back in 2018, I started recording songs over the prison telephone. The phone was all I had—no microphone, no recording equipment, no way to play a beat while I rapped, and no way to hear what I sounded like. But just having access to a shared wall phone was a huge change in my life. Until 2016, Death Row prisoners in North Carolina were allowed only one ten-minute phone call *a year*. We had that one call in December so we could wish our loved ones happy holidays, and that was it. What I am doing now, recording and releasing music, just wasn't conceivable until we started getting regular phone access.

Before I started recording, I had almost never shared my music. I wrote my rhymes for myself. It was my good friend Mu'min (Jason Hurst) who sparked the push. He came to visit me in my cell one day and saw me searching through a couple of large manila envelopes. When I got down on my knees and dug out some more envelopes, Mu'min asked what I was doing. I told him I was trying to find a rhyme. "Are these envelopes filled with songs?" he asked. "Yeah," I said. So then he asked, "Why do you keep them?" I looked at him like he was crazy. "What do you mean why do I keep them? I'm not gonna throw 'em away. They're my songs. I wrote them." "Yeah," he said, "but what good are they if nobody hears 'em?" Those words stuck with me.

Alim Braxton rapping on the prison phone.
Drawing by fellow Death Row resident,
Cerron T. Hooks.

He was right. What good are my songs if they're stuffed in envelopes under my bunk and nobody ever hears them?

I was scared at first. I talked to Mu'min about it several days later and told him my fears. As long as nobody heard them, I could always hold on to my dreams. In my dreams I made it as a successful MC. In my dreams, I was one of the best that ever did it. In my dreams, I could hold on to the belief that I was somebody special. But if I put my lyrics out there and nobody even noticed them, or if they said I was wack or even merely okay, then all my dreams would be destroyed. I would be forced to face the reality of being just another nigga in prison. I couldn't face that. But Mu'min, a white guy from West Virginia and not a typical hip hop fan, convinced me to give it a shot. He said, "But what if you really are as good as you believe you are? There's only one way to find out." So I sucked it up and dove in. Hopes, dreams, and all.

Mu'min inspired me to start sharing my rhymes, but I have to give a special shout-out to my man Stacey Tyler, who goes by Sabur. Sabur is my best friend. He's my confidant, adviser, and in-house producer. He's heard every rhyme I've got, multiple times. He's my number-one supporter and biggest fan on the inside. I can't give him enough credit. He's just as much a part of this as I am. On top of all that, Sabur is an innocent man on Death Row and one of the best people I've ever met in my life. So I'm not just doing this for myself. I'm doing it for Sabur and other people who don't have a voice, who can't generate attention for themselves. Allah is my witness: if I can get this music rolling like me and Sabur believe we can, then any shine I get is going to be used first and foremost to pursue justice for Sabur. The crazy part about it, is I'm gonna miss the hell out of him when he's gone!

In 2016, I met Michael Betts II. He was an audio technician who recorded me speaking monologues over the phone for an exhibition at Duke University called *Serving Life: ReVisioning Justice*. I called Michael a few weeks after we first spoke and asked if he could record me rapping. My intention was to attract a producer who could make a beat around my rhymes. After Michael posted some of my rhymes online, I was able to get the attention of a local producer who put a beat to my song, "Round My Way." I didn't get to hear the finished product until after it was released, and I wasn't pleased with the quality of the production—especially the distortion in my vocals. I talked to a few more local amateur producers, but no one seemed to know how to minimize the distortion. Still, I was convinced that it could be done. I felt like I was on the cusp of something.

It's been several years since I set out to record a hip hop album on Death Row. Let me tell you, it's been a loooooooong journey. I could fill a whole notebook with o's in writing the word "long" to describe this journey, and I'm not done yet. I don't even know where to start telling my story because everything is connected, and I feel like I'm leaving something out if I don't start from the beginning. But where to begin? I don't know, but I guess it should be with my mother.

Abortion or Adoption

MY MOTHER is a white woman named Marie Braxton. She was born in 1950 in Ayden, a small town in eastern North Carolina, the youngest of Harvey and Emma Lee Braxton's three kids. Harvey owned thirty-three acres of farmland and a house that had been handed down through the generations. When my mother was about eight, my grandfather went blind and could no longer manage the farm. My grandmother abandoned him and their three kids and ran off to Florida with another man. My grandfather couldn't take care of his kids due to his blindness, so my mother was placed in a foster home. After about a year, my grandfather's sister, Selma, adopted my mother, and my grandfather signed over ownership of the Braxton property to her. Selma and her husband, also named Harvey—Harvey Everett—became my mother's legal guardians and they raised her as their only child.

Harvey and Selma did well in managing the farm, and my mom didn't want for a thing. When she graduated from high school, they sent her to Raleigh to attend Meredith College to get a degree in English, and it was while she was in Raleigh that she met my dad. They fell in love and my mom got pregnant. When she broke the news to Harvey and Selma, they were outraged. Not only was she pregnant out of wedlock but the father was a Black man. They demanded she have an abortion and threatened to disown her if she refused. They gave her the money for the procedure, but she never went through with it. When the pregnancy was too far along to have an abortion, they sat her down and told her that she had to give the baby up for adoption. There was no way they could accept a Black child into the family. They were concerned about their status in the community. What would their friends and neighbors think if they consented to their daughter having sexual relations with a Negro? Even worse, my father had been arrested for trafficking heroin and was on his way to federal prison. Harvey and Selma refused to permit the baby to tarnish their reputation and swore they would cut her out of their will if she kept it. They pleaded with my mother. It wasn't too late—her pregnancy could still be concealed, and they could send her off to a home for unwed mothers in Durham. She could stay there until the baby was born, give it up for adoption, and then return to school the following semester. So she went to Durham and I was born on June 1, 1973, at Duke University Hospital.

After giving birth, my mom did indeed give me up for adoption. She returned to Ayden, but she couldn't get me out of her mind. She had fallen in love with me and now felt a gaping void in her life. Her love for me outweighed everything else—her parents' social standing, other people's opinions of her, a family inheritance. She remembered being in a foster home, unloved and unwanted, and couldn't allow her son to grow up feeling the same way. She loved me, and it didn't matter what anyone thought.

Social Services had told her that she had six months to change her mind about the adoption, but it didn't take near that long. She told her parents of her decision and then called a friend from Meredith College, Jean Merritt Saunders, who picked her up and took her to her mother's house in Louisburg. Jean's mom said she could stay with them until she found a job and a place to live, and the next day they came and got me. Not long after, my mom got a job at the Howard Johnson motel in Raleigh, and we moved into a room there. At the time, my crib was just a dresser drawer, but when she got her first check she bought me a real crib, and we never left Raleigh again.

My mom did manage to resume some semblance of a relationship with Harvey and Selma. However, she never told them about my crimes or that I was on Death Row. Instead, she told them I was doing great, that I had gone to college and was living a successful life. I understood and never felt for a moment that she regretted having me. I knew she just didn't want to give them the satisfaction of feeling that she should've listened to them.

When Selma died, she willed everything to her husband, Harvey. He ended up remarrying within a year or so, and he willed everything to his new wife and her adult son. His new wife died before he did, but when Harvey died around 2005, he left the farm and all of the properties he had acquired to his second wife's adult son and a stepson who had no connection to the family. In addition, Harvey had over $250,000 in cash in the bank, and he left that to his next-door neighbor. True to their word, they left nothing for my mother.

My biological grandad, Harvey Braxton, died when I was a little kid. We visited him a few times, and I knew in his heart he accepted me as a grandson. The funny thing is I look like him. He was tall, big, strong, and bald, just like me!

Bigger Lover

Mama had a rough start her early years was the tough part
You'da thought it would've left her with a scuffed heart
By the time she was nine her Daddy was blind
And her Mama skipped town, left her babies behind
So Mama got thrown in an orphanage
Left to rot with all the misfortunates
But Lord have Mercy, Ma won't rot
She was eventually adopted by her own aunt
Saved from a childhood of poverty
Her aunt inherited all of her Daddy's property
Thirty-three acres and a small farm
A big white house he had it all pawned
Signed over to his sister when he went blind
With the hope of keepin' it within the family line

Her aunt got married it was all great
All of Mama's burdens turned to being small weight
Soon she graduated and headed to college
Came to Raleigh, went to school she was getting that
    knowledge
But Mama hit the family with a backhand
When she told 'em she was pregnant by a Black man!
Jaws hit the floor, God almighty
Wish Mama coulda heard, "It's alrighty"
But they didn't play frolickin' with Negroes
Pick one of two choices but the kid goes
They would pay for an abortion or either adoption
But she knew that neither choice was not even an option
So they kicked her to the curb like white trash
Cut her out the will and had her rights slashed
With just God and a dark cloud up above her
She was branded in the world as a nigger lover!

Baby of a Caucasian mother
Instead of love her they let her suffer and labeled Mama as a
    nigger lover
But my Mama is a bigger lover
They didn't trust us, wouldn't hug us
Instead of love us they'd rather cuss us
And labeled Mama as a nigger lover
But my Mama is a bigger lover

I grew up in West Raleigh, a little bitty hood known as
    Kentwood
The projects where the reefer and the rent good
1142 on Clanton Street
Trapped between white bread like sandwich meat
The house with the screen door broken on it
Beside Tahalia and her Mama 'fore they started smokin'
It was just me, Chris, Mama, and Keisha
After Chris and Keisha's Papa had died from a seizure
Three half-breeds with a white mother
At school for our race they would write "other"
Mama had the weight of the world on her

Marie Braxton in her home, Raleigh, NC, July 18, 2021.
The framed photo in the center shows (*left to right*) Alim,
Keisha, Chris, and Marie Braxton. The pillows show Keisha
Braxton, who passed away in February 2020. Photo by
Mark Katz.

All alone 'cause her own people disowned her
Head held high she was unbroken
If there was pain in her heart it was unspoken
Outside the world was a sad place
But come home Mama greet us with a glad face
And anytime we fought she would intervene
Remind us nothing in the world ever come between
The bond of a true mother, sister, brother
'Cause in this world all we'll ever have is one another
Always stick together, that's what Mama say
Help your brother and your sister, that's what Mama say
Celebrate every day like a holiday
And remember we will always be a family

Baby of a Caucasian mother
Instead of love her they let her suffer and labeled Mama as a
    nigger lover

But my Mama is a bigger lover
They didn't trust us, wouldn't hug us
Instead of love us they'd rather cuss us
And labeled Mama as a nigger lover
But my Mama is a bigger lover

Forty-five years later and we as strong as we ever been
Despite all the drama that the devil send
I still got my Mama and my brother there
Still got lil' sis and some others now
Got a Chris Jr. and a little Rome
Teasha and Aniyah, Mama got a bigger home
Keisha got bad health but a good soul
Chris drink too much but got a heart of gold
And I'll be damn if I ain't end up on Death Row
But Ma swear she ain't got one regret though
Her kinfolks died round '05
Stayed true, ain't leave Mama one dime
Quarter mil in the bank and her daddy's land
Left it all to the neighbors and another man
But Mama ain't bat not one eye
Kept her chin to the sky, head held high
And you can tell her what you want when you speakin' of her
For every little bit of hate she's a bigger lover!

Baby of a Caucasian mother
Instead of love her they let her suffer and labeled Mama as a
    nigger lover
But my Mama is a bigger lover
They didn't trust us, wouldn't hug us
Instead of love us they'd rather cuss us
And labeled Mama as a nigger lover
But my Mama is a bigger lover

Being Biracial

ALL MY LIFE I've identified as Black. I learned from a young age that there weren't many options. At school it was Black, White, or Other. Most of my friends were Black, and I grew up in predominantly Black neighborhoods. Everyone told me I was Black. Didn't seem like I had much of a choice. Black people would say, "If you got some Black in you, you're Black. You ain't half nothing, you Black!" I liked the acceptance. It was like I was initiated into all the secret societies of Black people. I got to see stuff white people would never see.

Yet I knew the secret societies of white people, too. I was raised by a white mother. I have a white aunt and uncle. White grandparents. My mama is from a small North Carolina farming town. We're talking about down South, country white folks. I spent a summer when I was fifteen living with my grandma in Ayden. She'd play country music all day on her little kitchen radio, and her favorite was George Jones. My uncle Jimmy was the stereotypical redneck. He chewed tobacco. Always wore a cap. Drove a pickup with a gun rack in the window. Loved to go hunting and had the thickest country accent you could imagine. Some of my friends would assume that Jimmy sits around hating Black people all day. Truth is that for the most part Jimmy ain't thinking about Black people. He's thinking about the weather, the crops, hunting season, chopping firewood. I know my uncle Jimmy loves me to death. To him, I ain't Black, or mixed, or nothing. I'm his nephew.

But racial prejudices and distrust still exist. White folks have said the most bigoted comments in front of me because they don't think of me as one of *those people*. At the same time, I can be with my Black friends and hear them say stuff about white people, and it's just as bigoted. Nobody's paying me no mind. It always makes me feel like I don't know where I belong. No matter how accepted I am among Black people, or by my white family, I'm still a part of both, and it always feels like a betrayal to either race to acknowledge that. I like to identify myself as biracial because it's empowering. Being biracial is the story of who I am, the conflict that shaped me and that has propelled me throughout my life. It's my way of saying to everyone that you can't define me. Even though I've shouted it countless times, it's the cry that almost never gets heard. When you're biracial and live in a world defined by Black and white, you often get overlooked.

I've been able to work out a lot of my issues with race and self-hate by writing about them in my rhymes. I'll share some and try to explain what I mean:

> You couldn't understand my hate my pain
> I explain my life through music
> What I write is therapeutic
> Even the shrinks couldn't diagnose me
> Nobody knows me homie

These lines are from my song, "If I'm a Killer." The hate is self-hate. I grew up hating my identity, feeling ashamed of my racial makeup. The pain comes from not belonging to either race. Feeling rejected and despised by whites and mocked and teased by Blacks, as if my membership was always revocable. In that song I also talk about how my mother's family rejected me, how they wanted my mother to abort me or give me up for adoption because my father is Black:

> The whole world hate me, tell me what was my guilty sin?
> Just my light brownish milky skin?

So facing death ain't new in the womb they wanted to kill me
    then
Which means I've been on Death Row ever since my mom was
    pregnant
I'm an outcast born rejected.

In another song, "Cemetery in the Flesh," I refer to the first time that I became conscious of the fact that my mother was white, and by that, I mean not just the color of her skin but what whiteness represented to Black people—racism, slavery, hatred, discrimination:

Still you can't imagine what the feeling was like
When it was pointed out to me that my mama was white
Which explained why my skin was light.

I was in fourth or fifth grade. My mom had to come to school for a parent-teacher conference and a little Black girl asked me who was that lady I was with. When I told her that was my mom, she looked at me in disbelief and exclaimed, "Your mama is white?!" To me she was simply Mama. But when I realized that other people saw her as white, I felt ashamed:

White folks would stare and whisper hushed words
Mama paid it no mind like it was unheard
But the words would sting they said things like "nigger lover"
And "half-breed" like I didn't understand the hate
I can't lie I cried tears by my lonely
Nobody knows me
I'm an outcast, society freak
Nobody speaks my language

I also talk about being biracial in songs like "3 Words," "A Bigger Lover," "Goodbye to the Good Guy," and "God's Mercy," to name a few. By the grace of Allah I've been able to find self-acceptance and self-love and now I am proud of my racial identity. I fully embrace it. My songs are my testimonies, my scars, my journey.

Hymn of H.I.M. (He Is Me)

Who could've seen it but the prophets?
The gun, the weed, the projects
A young seed blooms inside the darkness
With no light his future unfolds
A broken rose his soul's cold
He dies as he grows with eyes closed
In blindness, walkin' alone searchin' divineness
A heavy load a narrow road how will he find it, criminal
    minded?
None of the teachers could reach him the preachers scold him
    but couldn't show him the role of guidance
All alone in confinement
They point their fingers at him but he didn't mold the
    environment

He's just a crossbreed, the offspring of contradiction
The legacy of nigger lynching
The pedigree of mixing enemy blood
A four-century taboo that pretends to be love
Or was it lust for forbidden fruit?
'Cause when sin is at the root the offshoot's surely corrupted
Plus his skin was tainted
The color of flesh that men degraded
He's an outcast society's waste the mixed-race half-breed
Biracial, so many labels for this bad seed
Is he Black or mulatto?
Society still calls him a nigger he drinks liquor from the bottle
To soothe the wounds that scarred him
Temporary escape from hell his heart hardens
His every day is a struggle
Who can relate to this young man who's troubled?
There was his father who never loved him
Fuck it his mother would hug him
But hugs don't erase the drama
How could he face his problems and explain that he was
    ashamed of his own persona
His flesh and blood and his own Mama
He inhales a moment of hope from the blunt smoke
But it's only temporarily
Slowly reality begins to surface
To face defeat, he feels so purposeless
He yearns for guidance but this cold world is merciless
Feelin' so worthless his heart races and rages with wildness
They never see the lonely tears he wastes in his silence
Placed in confinement they label him violent blamed for
    defiling
Society's laws of what they call goodness and piety
They chain his wrists up in iron rings
Claim that he's vomit to humanity a monster or some kind of
    thing
He only mimicked what he learned from them
I ask why as he wait to die as I cry singin' this hymn of him . . .

Jeannie

DO YOU KNOW what is never talked about enough when it comes to the subject of incarceration? Love. It's taboo, unworthy of being acknowledged. The prevailing attitude is that anyone who falls in love with a prisoner is stupid. The prisoner is seen as incapable of love. To recognize someone as having feelings is to acknowledge their humanity, and it's hard to imprison people that you empathize with. This is how people thought about slaves. Black people were seen as subhuman, like they couldn't have feelings. Slaves used to "jump the broom" to get married, but to white people this was derided as some primitive imitation of a real wedding. If I tell someone that Jeannie is my wife, I get a similar response. My marriage isn't a real marriage in their eyes, and our love is less important, less significant than they imagine their own loving relationships to be. Yet I know that what I have with Jeannie is something realer than most people will ever experience.

I'm usually guarded about my love life because I don't want to open myself up to ridicule and scorn. I know how relationships like mine are regarded. But I want to write about it because I need to put it on record that I am a living, breathing human being. That I have a need to love and be loved and to share that connection of the hearts that all humans crave. I'm happy to say that I have found someone that I love and who loves me in return. I am so fortunate to have Jeannie as my wife.

Jeannie was the original inspiration to record my rhymes. When we reconnected and fell in love in June 2018, she became the motivating factor for everything I did. I wanted to take care of her, to honor her, to make her proud, and to let the world know how important she was to me. When I first started recording—no, before that—I told her I was going to record an album and make a million dollars and take care of her. She told me that she just wanted me to love her. Of course, I do love her, but I want to be able to provide for her, too. I want people to know that I love this woman so much that I work my ass off every day on Death Row. She assured me that I didn't have to do that. For her it's more about being faithful and honest and committed, making her feel secure and important.

Every single day, Jeannie is my confidant and my supporter. She gives me advice, and she believes in me 100 percent. She tells me all the time that I am her favorite rapper. "You just say that because I'm your husband," I tell her. She says, "No, that's not the only reason." "Well, what else then?" I ask. "Because I love your music," she says. From day one, Jeannie has believed in me and supported me and listened to my dreams. When I share good news with her, she says, "That's great, honey. I knew you would do it." And I smile. She always makes me feel good. And when I suffer a setback, she reassures me that everything is gonna be okay. She helps me make sense of it all, brush the dirt off, and get back to work. She is my motivator, comforter, and best friend. I share everything with her. There is no way this story would be complete without her. So it's worth telling the story of our love.

I first met Jeanne in 1991, but it took twenty-seven years for us to reconnect after unimaginable tragedies in both our lives. We got married on June 27, 2019. We married over the phone—it was nothing that required official approval or government acknowledgment. We did it to please Allah first and foremost because we didn't want to engage in an amorous relationship (even if it was noncontact) without being married first. I also wanted her to know that I was serious about my commitment, that I honored her and valued her and was eager to make her my wife in the eyes of Allah, the true Witness and Judge. We are allowed to have an actual ceremony, which we may still do one day, but I didn't want to get bogged down in paperwork and bureaucracy. I got Sabur and another brother to stand by me at the prison phone as witnesses as we married.

When I first met Jeannie in 1991, I was eighteen and she was fifteen. I recollected that first meeting in my song, "Emerald Vase":

> The first time I caught sight of you
> Who would've knew that over twenty years later you would be
>   my down chick and my rider too
> I walked up and said "hi" to you, something most guys were
>   shy to do
> But being the case I was a young smooth player with a talk
>   game, tell me what was I to do?
> You smiled and I almost stuttered
> Usually cool but now my heart fluttered
> From the look in your eyes it's like you saw right through me
>   and truly I can't recall another word I uttered
> But God must've saved me from making a blunder
> It's crazy because you chuckled and gave me your number
> I had intentions on my mind of making you my lady by
>   summer
> I still remember when I called you for the first time
> And your Mama told me not to call you after nine
> I told her "Yes, ma'am," and I won't the type that says "Yes,
>   ma'am"
> But truth be told you had a strong influence on my soul to
>   make me wanna be the best I can
> I called you again, we talked then and you were so sweet
> But after that, the streets called and I went all-in with both feet
> And I was so deep in that street life and you were so focused
>   and smart
> And I thank God you never got to know me 'cause I'da
>   probably broken your heart
> Now here I am after all these years and God's slowly cleaned
>   up my slate
> And both of us have come full circle, now tell me this is not
>   fate!

Tell me this is not God's Plan, tell me this is not Grace
Tell me this is not something rare to find like an Emerald Vase!

We reconnected through Facebook in 2018. I've never used Facebook my-self, but my sister Keisha created a page for me to share news about me with family and friends. Once it was up, I started to get friend requests. I asked her to tell me the names, and one of them was Jeannie Bunch. I only ever knew one Jeannie. I wondered if that was her. "Is she fine?" I asked Keisha. Keisha looked at her photo and said, "Yeah, she's pretty." Keisha then started rattling off information from her profile. "She has three kids, two boys and a girl, she went to Broughton High School and then NC Central. She's self-employed." I stopped her. "Is she married?" "No, she's not married." "Well, does she have a man?" "It says that she's single." "Okay, look, Keisha. Can you send her a message? Ask her if she used to live over by Cameron Village in the early '90s." She sent the message and within seconds she had a re-sponse: "Yep, that's me." I said, "Oh hell! Keisha, that's her. That's her! What am I gonna do? I gotta get up with her. We got to figure out something." Kei-sha was like, "Chill man, I got you. Let me handle this. I'm your wingman." I said, "My wingman? What you know about being a wingman?" She said, "Ask your brother. I used to be Chris's wingman all the time." I just laughed and told her to get me Jeannie's number. Sure enough, the next day she had the number. I never even inquired about another woman on my friends list. I just wanted to talk to Jeannie!

I called her up and reintroduced myself and then went right into telling her about some of my accomplishments since I'd been in prison. How I'd surrendered my life to God and accepted Islam. How I was a prayer leader now and delivered a weekly sermon and taught Ta'lim, or Islamic Study, each week. I also mentioned that I cowrote a play called *Count* and had several more positive endeavors that I was working on.

She said that was nice, but had a question: "So, when are you getting out?" I felt myself shrink to the size of an ant. "Uh, you don't know about my situation?" "No, I don't," she said. "Oh my. I'm sorry. I thought everybody knew. Um, er. I . . . I'm so sorry to have to tell you this, but I'm on Death Row." My heart was pounding. I was afraid that she wouldn't want to speak to me again. "Oh, I didn't know. I'm so sorry to hear that. If you don't mind me asking, what happened?" My heart dropped. "You mean, what happened for me to get the death penalty, or what happened for me to be locked up in the first place?" She didn't seem to know how to respond, so I asked, "You didn't know that I've been locked up all this time?" "No, I didn't," she answered. I just wanted to crawl up inside myself and hide. "This is so humiliating," I said. "I thought everyone knew. I'm sorry, I wasn't expecting this." "It's okay," she said. "You don't have to talk about it." "No, that's not it," I said. "I just didn't want my second chance at making a good impression to turn out like this. I feel awful. I wanted you to hear about all the positive things I've been doing, and now you have to hear about the absolute worst things. I'm just so embarrassed." "You don't have to be embarrassed," she said. "I'm not judging you or anything. I just didn't know." "Thanks for picking my face up," I said. "I don't have a problem telling you. So let's start from the beginning."

As if on cue, just when I told her about my death sentence, the recording announced that I had sixty seconds remaining on the call. After we hung up, I wanted to go to my cell and bury my head under the covers. Even though she invited me to call again, I figured she was just being polite. But when I mentioned the whole ordeal to a couple of guys, they encouraged me to call her back. So I did. It was the next day, June 1, my birthday. We had a great conversation. I called her a third time and asked about her self-employed status. She mentioned that she makes dolls but had worked as a nurse before hurting her leg and having to go on disability. I was curious. "What happened to your leg?"

As she told the story, I could feel the tension in her voice. She had noticed some pain. She used to walk a lot—she didn't have a car and her ex wouldn't let her get a driver's license—so she thought it was due to the walking. She went to the hospital one day because the pain was so bad. Finally, she said, "I remember waking up and the doctor told me I had to make a choice. All I could think about was my kids. I didn't even hesitate. It was my kids or my leg. I told him to amputate the leg." I was speechless. I felt my eyes water up, but at the same time something swelled in my heart. I knew how she felt telling me this. It was just like I felt just a couple days prior. Ashamed, worried someone might treat you differently after they know the truth about you. I wanted to tell her that it was okay. That I'm not gonna treat her differently. That I'm not gonna run away. Maybe that chance encounter all those years ago was never really chance at all. It was fate. I wasn't ready for her then. Nor was she ready for me. But Allah knew that we were meant for each other. I didn't tell her any of that right then. I just smiled in my heart and said to myself, "This is the one."

The next day I asked her how she would feel about being in a relationship with someone in my situation. I told her that I really enjoyed talking with her

Jeannie Bunch's high school yearbook photo, 1992.

on the phone and in those few days I found myself smitten. But I didn't want to delude myself and needed to know if I had a chance. She told me she'd never really thought about something like this before. She wasn't opposed to it but had to think about it. After about a week she said yes!

With Jeannie, I can honestly say I've found my other half. I've never met anyone like her. She is perfect for me. She has a great personality and a noble character. She listens to me. I can talk to her about anything. And she believes in God. In fact, she accepted Islam on March 31, 2019, ten months after we reconnected. I love her and respect her and feel so grateful to have her in my life. And she feels the same about me.

One of my goals is to be able to take care of her, to provide her with all the things she wants and needs. And to make it home to her so that we can be together and comfort one another in this life. That's my baby right there. I love me some Jeannie. I owe it all to Allah, and the best wingman ever—my sister Keisha (may Allah have mercy on her).

Marriage in Paris

I can imagine you being my wife, the true companion I need in
    my life
Your tender love and your comfort steady easing my strife
You see my struggle and you still wanna cuddle my soul
You're my blanket in this cold world to bundle and hold
I swear if I was able I'd take you wherever
We'd cruise the French Riviera, visit Fiji, whatever
I'd feed you toasted calamari cooked on a hibachi
Evening gowns to fit your body Gianni Versace
Designer clothes Burberry, Gucci, and Dereon
Louis luggage and Hermes clutches for you to carry on
First class, the only coach is the Coach you'll be clutchin'
Exquisite fabrics, furs, and mink you'll be mostly touchin'
Every morning you'd wake up to the smell of magnolias

And every night you go to sleep in my arms I would hold ya
Safe in my embrace so that nothing will harm ya
I'd be your knight in shining armor

And I'd treat you like an heiress, fly you to Paris
View the city from a terrace, buy you the rarest
Diamond ring of twenty carats, don't be embarrassed
When I bend down on one knee ask for your hand in marriage

Picture the view from the Eiffel Tower, visions of you in your
    finest regalia
Bridal gown by Vera Wang with the whitest of flowers
Your only daughter Tatiana your maid of honor
Chris and Quentin beaming with joy feelin' proud of they
    mama
Extended table filled with food like we feeding a banquet
Full orchestra setting the mood and the feeling is sacred
Fireworks ignite in the City of Lights
As you whisper in my ear that you with me for life
Crowds of bystanders staring in admiration
The whole scene lookin' like a coronation
My queenie, my Jeannie my every fascination
Baby you are my inspiration

Despite the fact that I'm low as a peasant who can't give rubies
    or gold
As a present
What God has given to us baby's the holiest blessing
The realest love that can't be purchased or bartered or sold
The fact that you found the other part of your soul
Contentment and commitment you truly can cherish
While everything else in this world will eventually perish
I will still be by your side when there's nothing that's left
For better or for worse and through sickness and health
I will be there for you baby no matter the weather
We can make it through whatever or any endeavor
Just you and me no matter what we encounter together
Just say you'll be with me forever!

And I'd treat you like an heiress, fly you to Paris
View the city from a terrace, buy you the rarest
Diamond ring of twenty carats, don't be embarrassed
When I bend down on one knee ask for your hand in marriage

Alhamdulillah!

LHAMDULILLAH MEANS ALL PRAISE is due to Allah. For me, saying it is an act of remembering, not only with my tongue but with my heart. I say Alhamdulillah when I am joyful because it is a reminder that whatever is bringing me joy in that moment ultimately comes from Allah. Being constantly reminded of this as well as declaring it out loud keeps me grounded. If we don't remind ourselves that the good things come from Allah, then we will essentially forget Allah and instead praise the objects that bring us joy.

I say Alhamdulillah to express my gratitude for good news or kind words. I say it when I get a letter that lifts my spirits. One time I received five letters from Jeannie in a single day. Alhamdulillah! Another time I got a letter that told me that some college students had volunteered to help me with my social media presence. I ran over to Sabur's cell and read it out loud to him. I said, "Alhamdulillah!" And Sabur repeated after me, "Alhamdulillah!" When I got invited to speak to a university class, I said, "Alhamdulillah!" When my brother Chris said he was proud of me for what I've accomplished with my music, all I could say was thanks and Alhamdulillah, I was so overwhelmed.

Not long ago, I had to leave the prison briefly to see a doctor for a minor procedure. I got to smell some gas! That's prison slang for taking a road trip. It was amazing sitting in the car, a Ford Explorer. All I could say over and over in my mind was Alhamdulillah. I hadn't been in a vehicle for at least ten years, and it was something special just to be on the road. I was awed by the torque and acceleration. When the driver hit the gas for the first time, I felt an unexpected pull that drew me back into the cushiony seats, more comfortable than anything I had sat in for twenty-nine years. Alhamdulillah! It was wintertime, and as I looked out at the bare trees, I thought about how Allah has created a season for their leaves to die and a season for them to be brought back to life. He is giving us signs to read right in creation, and it's proof that we too will be raised from the dead in the season that He has appointed for the Resurrection. Again, I thought, Alhamdulillah!

I say Alhamdulillah during my darkest times as well. In the summer of 2020, I was unjustly put in solitary confinement after many years with no infractions. I raged and despaired. But then I thought, maybe there is wisdom in my being on lock-up right now. I can spend this time writing and recording my inner thoughts and ideas, because maybe I'll never have time alone like this again. Especially if my music blows up! Every day will be busy, busy, busy. I was reminded of a verse in the Qur'an: "And so (the disbelievers) planned, but Allah is the Best of Planners." In other words, although the prison administration planned to shut me down and kill my work, Allah's plan was for me to use this period of isolation for another aspect of the work. When you experience evil or injustice, look at it through the lens of Allah and realize that He has a plan and a purpose in everything, and His plan is the Best of Plans. Alhamdulillah!

Saying Alhamdulillah keeps me humble and hopeful. Whatever I accomplish, whatever good things happen to me, whenever I see light in this world of darkness, I realize that all praise belongs to Allah. Whatever He has given me belongs to Him. He just lets me use it and when I die everything returns to Him. Alhamdulillah!

One Who Has Knowledge

ONE DAY IN 1998 OR '99, I was sitting in my cell and was looking at a list of Muslim names. I came across the name Alim, and right out the gate I liked the way it looked: عليم. I liked the spelling and the individual letters. I liked the way it sounded after rolling it off my tongue a few times. I didn't know anybody who had the name, and when I learned what it meant, I knew right away that it described me perfectly. It means one who knows or has knowledge. For me, learning something new is like tasting good food. It's delightful and pleasing, and it makes me desire more. I had been on my path to Islam since the early 1990s, but I didn't want to be so audacious as to name myself. I wanted a sign that this was the right name for me. A name is important. It's a precious gem. Besides, I wasn't sure if I could take on this name. A few years before I had decided to call myself Qur'an and an Arab Muslim told me that I couldn't call myself Qur'an. Just like I couldn't call myself Allah.

While I was looking at the list of names, a Christian friend named Renwick came to my cell door and peeped in the window. We were both on max lock-up, but he was out for his one hour of indoor recreation. I told him I was reading a list of Muslim names, and he asked if he could see it. I slid it to him through the side crack in the door and after scanning it for about five seconds he pointed to the word "Alim." "How you say that name right there?" I pronounced it for him: "Ah-leem." He looked to the right side of the paper and asked me if this was the definition. I told him yeah, and he said, "Well, that's you right there. That's your name." I was surprised and asked him why he thought it should be my name. "Because it is. It says, 'One who has knowledge,' and that's you. You *are* Alim." I told him I appreciated it, but I wasn't ready to choose a name right then.

About two weeks later, my friend Elrico Fowler moved to the block, and every day when it was time for his hour of recreation, he would come to my door and we would build. (Building is more than just having a conversation — it means we're adding to each other's knowledge.) We talked about religion, politics, history, race, science. I was an avid learner. I spent almost all my money on books. I bought textbooks on biology, chemistry, and physics. I purchased a science and technology encyclopedia. I had a geographical dictionary. I studied religion. I bought tons of books on Black history and race in America. I wanted to understand how Congress worked, how laws were passed, what the Electoral College was, so I bought books about the political system. I studied the dictionary. I taught myself about the Federal Reserve and interest rates and the stock market. I studied communism. If it existed and I heard of it and didn't know what it was or how it worked, I would study it until I understood it. I remember back then people were talking a lot about the Palestinian-Israeli conflict, and I was clueless. I would read the paper every day trying to figure it out. I would be confused by phrases such as "Palestinian Christians" and "Israeli Arabs." I didn't understand why they were fighting each other. But I read about it every day until I finally started to understand. That's how dedicated I was to knowledge.

A few weeks after my conversation with Renwick, Elrico came up to my door and said: "Akh, I know they call you Rome, but I was wondering how come you don't have a Muslim name." I told him I just hadn't found one yet. He said, "Well, I've been thinking about it, and brother, you have a lot of knowledge. I want to know if I can call you Alim because in Arabic, Alim means 'one who has knowledge.'" This was beyond coincidence. This was the name I had chosen. Renwick said I was Alim, and now, here was Elrico

Book list

<u>Crescent Imports</u>

12-0002 Arabic/English Dictionary Hans Wehr Dictionary New Edition - $45.00

12-0010 Teach Yourself Arabic - $15.50

15-0003 The Autobiography of Malcolm X - $7.95

15-0015 Sex and Race (3 Volume Set) - $50.00

15-0017 Breaking the Chains of Psychological Slavery - $10.00

15-0029 Before the Mayflower - $17.95

15-0028 Nelson Mandela - Struggle is My Life - $15.95

15-0055 The Destruction of Black Civilization - $19.95

15-0073 Life and Times of Fredrick Douglas - $15.95

15-0085 Afrocentricity - $10.95

15-0089 They Came Before Columbus - $25.00

15-0100 Black Robes White Justice - $15.95

15-0157 The Origins of Race and Color - 8.95

15-0185 How Europe Underdeveloped Africa - $12.95

<u>Larousse and Chambers</u>

ISBN: 0-7523-0010-5 Larousse Dictionary of Science and Technology - $45.00

ISBN: 0-7523-5008-0 Larousse Dictionary of World History - $18.95

ISBN: 0-7523-0005-9 Larousse Dictionary of North American History - $8.95

ISBN: 0-7523-0008-8 AB Larousse Dictionary of Beliefs and Religions - $14.95

<u>Tahrike Tarsile Qur'an</u>

Sahih Bukhari Volumes 1-9 (Hardback) - $105.00

Al-Kafi Volumes 1-12 (Paperback) - $120.00

One of many lists of book requests sent by
Alim Braxton to his mother. From an undated
letter to Marie Braxton.

saying the same thing. I felt like the name was meant for me, and I've been Alim ever since.

Our souls are created by Allah, and He names everything He creates. In this life our parents give us a name at birth, and that is what we are known by in this world. But I wonder if on the Day of Judgment, when the Creator calls us, will He address us by the name that we were known by in this life, or will He call us by our true name, the name that our souls will recognize as soon as it is called? I feel (and Allah knows best) that Alim is the name that He and the angels call me. It's the name I always use when I refer to myself or if I'm having an internal dialogue and I call myself by name. It's always Alim.

Alhamdulillah, that's how I got the name Alim!

My Creative Process

WHEN I WRITE RHYMES, most of the time I start with a topic or an idea, or even just a phrase. For example, in the case of "A Bigger Lover" I wanted to write a song about my mom and tell my family's story. I started with the phrase "nigger lover," which my mom got called because she was a white mother of Black children. When you hear the chorus, it might seem like I started with the phrase "bigger lover," but that actually came later:

> Mama is a bigger lover
> They didn't trust us wouldn't hug us
> Instead of love us they'd rather cuss us
> And labeled Mama as a nigger lover, but my Mama is a bigger
> lover

For my song "It Ain't Just Me," I started with the phrase "just us," which sounds like "justice," which then became, "It ain't just me, it ain't just us." I used that line to talk about injustice in society, like police killing unarmed Black people. You might think that "justice" led to "just us," but like in "A Bigger Lover," it was the other way around.

Sometimes I don't have a specific idea or topic, and I'll find it as the rhymes come. In those cases, I usually sit on my bed with my clipboard in my lap. I have my ink pen in my right hand, and I start tapping out a beat on the clipboard with the side of my fist and the ink pen. I'm looking for a rhythm or a groove. As I'm tapping, I sound out a melody. Once I'm feeling the rhythm, the melody becomes syllables, like "da da da." I just keep on repeating that cadence until a sentence replaces the syllables. Once I got that first line I just keep on building from there. I start thinking about what word I'm going to use to rhyme with the last word of the first line, and then what the fill-in words are going to be to lead me to that word. I also like to add extra rhymes inside the bar as well. I have to write everything down, though, because I will forget it real fast. By the time I've finished a song the page is filled with a bunch of edits, usually crossed out words or words in parentheses. A parenthesis usually means that I'm not sure about keeping it, but I'm not getting rid of it yet. But once I mark through it, it's gone for good. I always write in ink, and I often write alternative words or phrases above others. Here's the draft of "It Ain't Just Me." Compare it to the final version. This is the first time I've shared a draft of one of my songs. I *never* let anyone see stuff like this!

It Aint Just Me

it aint ~~they~~ mistreat and distrust us / *oppress me when* *they that hurts us*

It Aint Just Me, its Just Us / hurt me then it hurts us
Is it just me or injustice?

first crush me then they crush us / handcuff me is how they cuff us

Boom Boom / Tap Tap / Boom Boom Boom Boom Boom / Tap Tap

They say its *But*
~~(Aint no)~~ justice. They got me feelin like its just me / all alone on the asphalt on the *neck up under*
~~(other~~ ~~side of)~~ *(bottom)* that knee / by myself in ~~them~~ *these* handcuffs / dont shoot I'm hollerin Hands up / *I got my*
I aint tryin to be MAN down, ~~spirit~~ *system* tellin me to men up / ~~they got no space in the boardroom~~ *for me*
White faces in the courtroom / with black robes sending black souls *in* to a lifetime in them
warped tombs / ~~folks'll die to get free speech, protest to get~~ *for that* ~~free press~~ / freedom of press,
~~freedom of speech~~ / whats freedom of speech? Whats freedom of press? / When the cop
my people
Free to kick a door down and shoot a women to death? (protesters get tear gassed)

Tell me if its just me / or is it justice that the poor rot and the wealthy always go free? /
DAs conceal evidence, and dont get punished one lick *bit* / *despite the fact that the innocent* while the innocent can serve 30
served *lost 30 years for that shit /*
years
I protest with my flesh / everyday I fit the profile to be killed the way that I dress / tell me if its just
(You cant hide the truth with that mask / when the lootin starts the shootin starts and protesters
or really if it aint just us / the same wrist they get a slap on they turn around and cuff us /
get gassed) As protesters get gassed / the whole nation in a chokehold, *friend* with I cant breathe on
they they
Tap my mask / if I fall asleep in the drive thru *tryin to send me to the big house,*
Tap I cant breathe from that tear-gas, cops got me in a chokehold / *blacks there by the bottle land* /
Tap locked arms on the frontline, eyes red from the tear ~~gassed~~ *gassed* / COVID'll turn a slow bid in these *parke...*
packed up in them small dorms COVID got my breath slow / *dorms*
~~they done turnt this here small bid to Death Row~~ *they tryin to turn this small bid to Death Row*

slowly unfolds
As the drama starts to unfold / meanwhile in a courtroom I stood to face the unknown /
Now the whole country's on fire /
view the world from myself *cop cars* *nation* *patience done been worn down*
As I sit alone in this cell / (police stations *get* fire bombed, the country burnin like hell / statues gettin torn
down *forward march no turnin back best believe it, its on now /* ~~hatred done been unmasked~~ *from*
racism being unmasked from hatred that's
been passed on / evidence before COVID that most people had a mask on / I dont know what the future's
like / if the lootin starts they might shoot tonight / without protest I might lose my rights
on the other hand I might lose my life

Draft of "It Ain't Just Me." Excerpt from a letter from
Alim Braxton to Mark Katz, October 18, 2020.

It Ain't Just Me

It ain't just me it ain't justice
It ain't just me
It ain't just me it ain't justice
It ain't just me
It ain't just me it ain't justice, they mistreat and distrust us
Oppress me, then hurt us, is it just me or injustice?
It ain't just me, it ain't justice
It ain't just me
It ain't just me it ain't justice

They say it's justice, but they got me feelin' like it's just me
All alone on that asphalt, neck up under that knee
By myself in these handcuffs, Don't shoot I got my hands up!
I ain't tryin' to be a man down, system tellin' me to man up!

No space for me up in the boardroom, white faces in the
    courtroom
In black robes sending Black souls to a lifetime in them warped
    tombs
What's freedom of speech? What's freedom of press?
When the cops free to kick a door down and shoot a woman to
    death!

It ain't just me it ain't justice
It ain't just me
It ain't just me it ain't justice
It ain't just me
It ain't just me it ain't justice, they mistreat and distrust us
Oppress me, then hurt us, is it just me or injustice?
It ain't just me, it ain't justice
It ain't just me
It ain't just me it ain't justice

I protest with my flesh!
Everyday I fit the profile to be killed the way that I dress
Tell me, is it just me or really though is it just us?
On they wrists they get slaps on, on my wrists they put
    handcuffs
My eyes burn from that tear gas, cops got me in a chokehold
Tryin' to send me to the Big House, Blacks there by the
    boatload
Packed up in them small dorms, COVID got my breath slow
They done turn this here small bid to Death Row!

It ain't just me it ain't justice
It ain't just me
It ain't just me it ain't justice
It ain't just me
It ain't just me it ain't justice, they mistreat and distrust us
Oppress me, then hurt us, is it just me or injustice?
It ain't just me, it ain't justice
It ain't just me
It ain't just me it ain't justice

As I view the world from my cell
Cop cars getting firebombed, the nation burnin' like hell
Patience done been worn down, statues getting' torn down
Forward march no turnin' back, best believe it, it's on now!
Racism being unmasked from hatred that's being passed on
Evidence before COVID that most people had a mask on
I don't know what the future's like, if the lootin' starts they
    might
Shoot tonight
If I don't protest I might lose my rights
On the other hand I might lose my life!

My Raleigh

GREW UP IN A neighborhood called Kentwood. It's public housing so I wouldn't advise you to go through there on a casual walk, but the surrounding area is nice, safe even. In my song, "A Bigger Lover," I say:

> I grew up in West Raleigh, a little bitty hood known as
> Kentwood
> The projects, where the reefer and the rent good
> 1142 on Clanton Street
> Trapped between white bread like sandwich meat.

The line "trapped between white bread" is an allusion to white wealth because Kentwood is surrounded by middle-class, upper-middle-class, and affluent white neighborhoods. You could go for a walk right off Western Blvd. and see some nice houses. You could keep walking to Kentwood Park, with its baseball/softball field, its tennis courts, playground, and frisbee golf course.

It's beautiful. Tons of nice homes, trees, creeks. Perfect place for a walk. My mom used to take us trick-or-treating there. Or you could leave Western Blvd. and turn on Gorman Street and walk from there to Avent Ferry Road. A lot of small communities along the way—Marcom Street Apartments, Parkwood Village, Pinewood Village, King's Court. I used to deliver newspapers on my bicycle along that route. If you turn off Western Blvd. onto Method Road, that would take you to a historic Black community. One of the first schools for free Blacks in North Carolina was there. There are greenhouses that belong to NC State nearby. The Islamic Association of Raleigh is there, too, though it wasn't there when I was growing up.

If you go to Hillsborough Street and walk through NC State's campus, you'll get to Pullen Park. Right across the street from Pullen Park on the other side of Western Blvd there's a greenway path. Paths go all over Raleigh and are traveled by joggers and people riding bicycles as well as by hikers enjoying the scenery. And right across the street from Central Prison is the sprawling Dorothea Dix Park. I'm teary-eyed right now just thinking about my city and all the beautiful places I used to go to. I took it all for granted, not even pausing to drink it in and enjoy the scenery. The pine cones and pine needles, the acorns and all the oak trees. The squirrels. The honeysuckle. I miss the fire bugs we used to catch and let go on summer nights.

I can probably name every business on both sides of Western Blvd. I remember Amedeo's, an Italian restaurant just down the street from where we lived on Clanton. We couldn't afford places like that back then, so I never ate there. Plus, Mama said she could make spaghetti at home. There was a barbershop right beside Amedeo's, but it was a white barbershop. There was a nightclub that had different names over the years: Shooters, Shooters II, and Kamikaze's. There was a Pizza Hut, a Pizza Inn, and a gas station on the corner. I'd been to those places or walked or drove by them countless times. Back in the day, there was a grocery store on the other side of Western Blvd. It was an A&P, and then it became a Save-A-Center. We used to take the grocery carts and push them back to Kentwood. Sometimes we'd ride in them down the hill on Neely Street. Or we'd take them to the basketball court, turn them on their side and put a big rock inside; and then we'd run and jump up on them so we could dunk on the basketball goal. Or we'd take the wheels off and make skateboards. Lots and lots of memories.

I've captured some of those memories in my music. In my song, "The Good Stuff," I reminisce about my childhood, a time "when I was innocent." Here's the first verse:

Sometimes I sit back and recline, review the thoughts from the
    back of my mind
And when I'm feelin' kinda low I go back in them times
And I remember all the good stuff
The family and neighborhood stuff, when I was innocent
I can see it all like I'm living it
The small things are so significant we can belittle it
We don't appreciate it till we're rid of it, then we'll be missing
    it
Wishing it would be right before our eyes again
I remember when we had them Sunday breakfasts
We'd go to Shoney's for the buffet, my head spint like *The
    Exorcist*
Crazy about them muffins and a demon for them cheese grits
Them French toast sticks and scrambled eggs smothered in
    cheese dip
I loved it when it used to be my turn at riding shotgun
Or sitting in the hatchback with Doc in Mama's Datsun
Playin' catcher in baseball wearing all my equipment
Or swimming at the Y on Thursday night that was
    contentment,
The good stuff

When I mention Doc, I'm talking about my brother Chris. As I say in a later verse, these are the things we take for granted later in life, the good stuff.

When my family left Kentwood, we moved to a house on Edmond Street, off Brookside Drive. We had a cat named Muffin, and man, I still love the cat and think about her today. My mom didn't like Muffin because she said she was mean and would bite and scratch, but I never had any problems with her. She also had several litters of kittens, which my mom didn't like either. But Chris, Keisha, and I claimed and named them all. Some of the ones I remember were Bizmark, Ace, and Romeo, who were my cats. Then there was Baby, Midnight, and Butterball. I loved all our cats. To this day if I see a black-and-white cat on TV, I'll say, "There goes Muffin!" I don't get to see cats in real life anymore. A few people in Central Prison say they've seen cats on the yard, but I haven't seen one since I've been here, and that's more than thirty years now. If I did see a cat, I'd probably try to bring it inside and keep it in my cell.

Undated Braxton family photo. *Clockwise from left*:
Marie, Alim (a.k.a. Jerome), Chris, and Keisha.
Courtesy of Marie Braxton.

I love Ruff Raleigh. I want young and upcoming musicians to feel proud
to say, "I'm from Raleigh!" I want people to talk about the food in Raleigh
like they talk about the steak-and-cheese sub from Philly or the barbecue in
Kansas City. I want the slang and the culture to be just as influential as New
York City's. Raleigh is growing. People from all over are moving here, but I
don't want the Black history and culture of this city to be lost or displaced by
affluence. You feel me? I want to exalt and preserve. A lot of places are being
lost to gentrification, and I want to say, "We were here, and we are here,"
before we aren't here anymore.

Descent into Crime

I HAVE FOND MEMORIES of my childhood growing up in Raleigh, but as I wrote in my song, "Unbreakable," it's also where I learned "to thug it properly." Stealing, fighting, and drinking were rites of passage in my neighborhood. My descent into crime didn't happen overnight. I got my feet wet shoplifting around the age of eleven. By the time I was sixteen I had gone to prison for two months for stealing a car. I soaked up more criminal knowledge while inside, and after my release, the front gate became a revolving door, with a dozen arrests and three additional stints in prison.

One of those stints was for stealing beer out of a convenience store called The Pantry. I mention it in my song, "Iqra." *Iqra* is an Arabic command meaning "Read!" It is said to be the first word revealed to Muhammad in the Qur'an.

> An ig'nant ass nigga who ain't never read a book
> Walk in the store everything getting took

> A dumb fuckin' crook but a nigga got heart
> Sent to the pen stealin' beer out the mini-mart!

True story. Me and my best friend ran out of The Pantry with two twelve packs. I had parked his Trans-Am behind a nearby Food Lion. We were gonna run out of the store, down the hill, across the parking lot and then jump in the car and pull off. What was I thinking? That's a marathon with two heavy twelve packs! And at the exact moment we stepped out of The Pantry a cop car was riding by. He saw us and hit the gas and chased us down through Food Lion's parking lot. As I tried to get away, I started throwing beers at the cop car, which was right on my heels. The cop actually knocked me down with his car! My friend got away, but I went to jail. It was August 13, 1991. I remember because it was another friend's birthday, and we were going to The Pantry to steal some beer for him. He was turning eighteen a few months after me.

In 1992, I was serving nine months in prison for parole violation and several other misdemeanor convictions. This was the longest time I had ever been away from home. When I returned, everything was different. I had to borrow some of my brother Chris's clothes, my social groups had been permanently altered, and of my two best friends, one was married with a kid and the other was in jail for murder. Hanging out with my younger brother and some of his friends, I found myself at the bottom rung of a new social order. All my life, Chris had been in my shadow, and now the roles were reversed. Keisha was fifteen, and all she wanted to do was stay in her room and talk on the phone with her friends about boys. I felt like I didn't belong. I wasn't needed or looked up to like I had been all my life. Chris had a job working at Bojangles and was getting a Social Security check each month because his father passed away when he was only four. That meant he had money. I had nothing.

There was a friend of Chris's, who I'll call R., who stayed in the same cul-de-sac as us. He was into deejaying and was real heavy into the Hit Squad, a hip hop collective that EPMD, Das EFX, K-Solo, and Redman were a part of. He'd just started growing dreads, and liked to wear all black: jeans, boots, hoodies, and a winter hat we call a toboggan in the South. I was home only about two or three days when he came over to the house with a pistol in his waistband. I had never seen or held a real gun in my life. I was in awe. I had been running in the streets doing petty crimes, mostly stealing and damaging property, getting into fights, drinking a lot of beer and cheap wine and liquor, smoking weed and occasionally selling a little. I'd been to jail multiple times, and to me this was stripes, dues paid to show and prove my street cred.

But I had never done anything serious. Never been around any hard drugs, never touched a gun. I was just a petty criminal. So when I saw R. with this pistol, I automatically felt like I had more right to be toting a gun than he did. I'd grown up in the projects. I'd been to prison. To my knowledge, this guy had never been arrested. I'd dropped out of school after getting kicked out at fifteen, yet I felt like he had surpassed me on the gangster ladder. I felt a twinge of envy. I wanted a gun. I at least wanted to hold one, put it in my waistband, and look at myself in the mirror. I was nineteen years old and fascinated with the idea of being a gangster.

He let me hold the gun, a nine-shot .22 revolver. It was big and heavier than I expected. I wanted to shoot it, just to say I'd shot a gun, so I went up-stairs, held it out my bedroom window and fired into the air. I was excited! After I gave him back the gun, I asked him a few questions, and to my utter disbelief he told me that he was a stick-up kid. R. was out there committing armed robbery? I didn't have the guts. I'd seen flyers posted in store windows warning potential bandits that armed robbery was punishable by a manda-tory seven years in prison. I'd just gotten out of prison, and there was no amount of money that I could imagine worth seven years of my life.

When I inquired more, he told me that he'd robbed pizza delivery men and taxi drivers. I had never even thought about that. In my mind robbery was robbing a bank. But when he described how easy it was to make a quick $500, he had my attention. By the time he left, I was all in. I made him prom-ise to take me on the next heist.

And that was December 19, 1992, only eight days after I had gotten out of prison. R. called me and told me to wear all black. We left my house on foot and walked about a mile to a pay phone on Capitol Blvd., and then he called a taxi. I was nervous, but excited. When the taxi pulled up, were we going to pull the gun out, take the money and run? I had no clue. I was following his lead. He'd done this before. I hadn't.

The taxi arrived. The driver was a woman. I was ready to abort the whole mission. I didn't want to rob no woman. But R. opened the door and got in the backseat and motioned for me to get in on the other side. What was I supposed to do? I felt like I couldn't back out now. I got in. She asked for our destination. She had a heavy accent. I later found out she was from Kenya. R. gave her a destination and we rode off. I watched the meter—it was getting expensive real quick. What if she suspected that we didn't have any money and just drove us straight to the police station? I kept glancing over at R. wondering when and where we were going to do it. We were approaching the downtown area. Cops would be everywhere.

Finally, R. reached inside his jacket, pulled out the pistol and put it on the floorboard right between my feet. He wanted *me* to do the robbery! Was this a test? I'd never done anything like this before. I was scared we were gonna get caught. I had to improvise, so I asked her, "Where are you going?" "You said Walnut Terrace, right?" she answered. I said, "Naw! Not Walnut Terrace, Washington Terrace. You know where that's at, right?" She looked at me in the rearview and said, "Washington Terrace?" I said, "Yeah," and she called it in to the dispatcher and changed direction.

As we pulled into Washington Terrace, I directed her to the middle of the neighborhood to a dark area in a semi-deserted parking lot. Once she parked, I picked up the pistol and became an actor in a movie. My job was to convince her that I would blow her head off if she didn't give me the money. I was very convincing. We made her get out of the cab, lay on the ground, and we took all her money and the taxi and drove off. We ditched the taxi a couple of blocks away and left on foot. We split the money, over $300 apiece. It was that easy.

I was all in. I committed several more robberies after that, but that first one I will never forget. The taxi driver's name was Susan Indula, and I would later be charged with robbing her, though only after I was in jail for murder. During my trial, she explained that she had come to this country seeking a better life for her and her five children. She had been a student at NC State and drove the taxi to provide for her kids. She broke down in tears several times as she told the jury how she had feared for her life, and how she was still afraid of me. She could not bring herself to make eye contact with me.

When I committed that crime, Susan Indula was nobody to me. I was just acting out a role. I never had any real intention of harming her, but that's not how she experienced it. When I heard her testimony, I realized that the role I had been playing was no act to her. I'd put a gun to her head. She begged me for her life. She thought she would never see her children again. As I listened to her speak, I imagined my own mother in her place, and I felt so terrible, so low, so despicable. I cried later that day when I was alone as I thought about the terror I'd inflicted on her. My eyes water now as I think about this woman. That was the first time that I truly, truly felt remorse for one of my crimes.

We Had Just Kidnapped a Man

AFTER ROBBING SUSAN INDULA IN DECEMBER 1992, I went on a spree. While the robberies were stacking up, the money wasn't—I never made as much as I did that first time. But then, on the night of February 12, 1993, R. asked me if I was down for doing another robbery. He showed me a sawed-off shotgun in an orange duffel bag, and I told him I was with it. My brother's friend, who I'll call K., was there and said he was in, too. We didn't have a plan but somehow we ended up on a corner in Washington Terrace, not far from where I'd committed my very first robbery.

After maybe ten minutes, a car pulled up. The driver got out, and we spontaneously decided to rob him. R. pulled the shotgun out and I checked his pockets. He had two keys, a joint, and a twenty-dollar bill. On impulse, I decided we should take his car. Rob took the keys and handed me the shotgun. I told the driver to get in the backseat. This was one of the worst decisions I've made in my life. My thinking was that if I just left him standing on the side of the street, he'd run to a pay phone and call the cops. He'd give them the make of the car and the license number, and we'd be caught in no time. So we drove around with him in the back seat, trying to figure out our next move.

I asked him his name. He told me it was Donald Bryant. I told him we wanted to use his car to do some robberies. That we weren't gonna hurt him, but we couldn't just let him go because he'd call the police and report his car stolen and then we'd go to jail. So he had two choices—he could ride with us and be a part of the robberies, or we were gonna put him in the trunk. I don't know why I said this. I suppose I was just trying to scare him because I had no intention of putting him in the trunk. But after the words came out of my mouth, they dictated what happened next—R. stopped and ordered Bryant to get in the trunk. I couldn't believe what was happening. We had just kidnapped a man and put him in the trunk of his own car. Suddenly, everything had gotten real. I was afraid that Donald Bryant might get killed. So I decided to hold on to the shotgun. As long as I controlled possession of the gun, I reasoned, no one was gonna get hurt.

There's an adage I learned in 2004 that means so much to me now: "The decisions you make today determine your tomorrow." I've asked myself countless times, why did I have to control the gun? Why didn't I just leave after we put Donald Bryant in the trunk? Even before that, when I robbed Susan Indula, why did I pick that gun up off the floorboard and put it to her head? Each evil decision I made led me to more evil decisions. I thought I was making the best decision each time, but in reality I was sinking deeper and deeper into evil. When I decided I wanted to do a robbery, I looked at it as a quick-fix solution for my money problems. When I picked that gun up off the floorboard, I felt like it was my only option to go through with the robbery because I didn't have taxi fare. I didn't leave because I felt like I had to be in control. I accepted the shotgun because I thought I *was* in control. With every decision I dug a deeper hole, and I didn't stop digging until I couldn't see any light above.

Why Didn't I Just Leave?

WHY DIDN'T I JUST leave at some point during that February night in 1993? The truth is that I was afraid I would look weak. I know now that it's not weak to walk away from something you don't want to be involved in. That it takes real courage to buck what others are doing. But I felt like I had to see this through, and I didn't have the courage or the strength to walk away. Not walking away was a pivotal decision that changed the course of my life forever. Like I said, the decisions you make today determine your tomorrow. What were the consequences of the decisions I made that night? Two deaths and two life sentences plus 110 years.

We hit the streets with two six-packs of Schlitz Malt Liquor Bull, a sawed-off shotgun, and four shotgun shells. Around 2 a.m., R. was ready to call it a night, but I felt like there was still more to be done. In my mind we'd risked too much to end the night broke, and I wanted money to at least rent a hotel room for a week. R. said, "Well, what you want to do then, rob this store?"

We were on Millbrook Road and happened to be riding by a Fast Fare convenience store. I had never robbed a store before. This seemed like we were upping the ante, but after kidnapping a man and holding him in the trunk for several hours, the stakes were already high. I looked over at K. to see what he thought. He shrugged like it was up to me. In an act of boldness I said, "I don't give a fuck, let's do it." Without another word R. pulled into a parking lot behind the store. K. and I each chugged down another beer to still our nerves. Without the semblance of a plan, we hurried toward the store.

I had the shotgun pressed close to my body with the extra shells in my Carhartt jacket pocket. We were both wearing dark hoodies and jeans. As we rounded the corner of the building and into the storefront lights, a long window gave us an open view of the inside. I noticed two people in the far aisle and no one behind the register. Keeping the shotgun concealed I mumbled to K. that I wanted him to go to the register and I was gonna circle around from that far aisle. I was thinking he would casually wait at the register as if he were a customer until I arrived with the shotgun. Of course, none of this was communicated. When we entered the store, K. went right and I went left with the shotgun still concealed. I had no idea what might be awaiting me. I had never done a robbery like this before, and the only references I had to draw on were from TV and movies.

As I circled around the back, one of the two people began to walk to the front of the store where K. was at. This man turned out to be the clerk. The person he left in the far aisle was a female customer. When I rounded the aisle, I raised the shotgun to waist level and told her quietly to get on the floor. She immediately complied. I noticed right away that she was wearing an expensive leather hooded jacket and a Gucci watch, which I ordered her to remove. As she handed me her belongings, I heard K. call out with a frantic cry, "Rome, help!" I looked up and saw K. and the clerk scuffling. I immediately made my way to the front of the store.

It was only later that I could make sense of what had happened. K. had gone to the register, opened it, and had started taking money out of it when the clerk arrived and attacked him. Since I hadn't brandished the shotgun for the clerk to see, he had no reason to suspect that this was an armed robbery. At least this is what I have concluded after years of reflecting on it. When I arrived and the clerk saw me with the shotgun, pandemonium erupted. He immediately began to yell in a language I could not understand—he was Nigerian—and he ran to the front window and began pounding on it with both fists to get attention. I started to panic and tried to regain control. I told him in a loud voice, "Shut the fuck up and get on the floor." But to no avail. He was still speaking in his language, so I raised the shotgun with the thought of firing a round in the ceiling to quiet him. Again, this was something I had seen done in movies. But when I pulled the trigger, nothing happened. I tried it again, cocking the hammer back with my thumb and squeezing the trigger. The hammer slammed forward but the gun did not fire. Now I really began to panic. I wasn't sure if the clerk noticed that the gun had misfired. If he did, maybe he would have the upper hand. He might have a gun hidden somewhere and then run to retrieve it. He could hold K. and me at gunpoint until the cops arrived.

I reached in my jacket pocket and quickly pulled out another shell and broke the shotgun down just like I had seen R. do earlier. The shell popped out and I put the other one in. I was nervous. Maybe the shotgun was just a prop and didn't even work. Unlike the .22 that I had used in previous robberies, I had never fired this gun. Never even seen it fired. I put the new shell in, cocked back the hammer and pulled the trigger again. I didn't even aim it. Didn't even look up to see where the barrel was aimed at. I was looking at the gun when I pulled the trigger, expecting it to misfire again.

BOOM! I almost dropped the gun. When I looked up, I saw the clerk seemingly being lifted off his feet and then falling to the floor. "Oh shit," I thought, "I must've shot him!" I didn't see any blood like in the movies, so I wasn't sure. I turned to K. and saw his mouth moving but no words were coming out. I realized that I was momentarily deafened by the shotgun blast. I looked back at the clerk on the floor. He wasn't moving but I still didn't see any blood. I turned back to tell K. to get the money, but he was gone and the front door was swinging. I thought they were gonna leave me, so I took off running out the store and jumped in the backseat with K. As my hearing came back, I heard K. yell, "Go! Go!" and we pulled off.

K. blurted out, "I can't believe you shot him!" "What?!" demanded R. "You shot somebody? What happened?" K. said, "Rome killed that muthafucka, man!" I was in shock. I didn't know what to say. "You think he's dead?" I asked K. "Hell yeah, he's dead. I can't believe you shot him!" We all let the gravity of the situation sink in as we rode for the next several minutes in silence. Everyone consumed by their thoughts.

Oh My God, What Have I Done?

I HAD JUST KILLED SOMEBODY. I never imagined that something like this would ever happen. What had I done? Would I be haunted and tormented by his ghost? What about my soul? Was I now doomed to hell? I had crossed a line that I could never uncross.

As I turned these thoughts over in my mind, R. pulled up to his mother's house and parked the car. He was done for the night. We could keep the shotgun. He was taking the leather coat and the Gucci watch from the woman I robbed. Later, I got them back and gave them to my girlfriend for Valentine's Day.

K. got behind the wheel. "What now?" he asked. "I don't know," I said. "We're probably gonna have to go on the run and get out of the state. Where you wanna go?" He wasn't sure. For some reason I said Delaware. I felt like I was acting out a script from a movie. I didn't know what to do, but on TV the bad guys always go on the run and leave the state. K. said we should get off the road and maybe get a hotel room for the night and figure out what we were gonna do in the morning. He pulled into a huge parking lot at a shopping center about 150 yards away from a hotel. We got out of the car and walked over to the hotel to see about renting a room, but they required ID. We didn't want our real names on record at the hotel, so we left and headed back to the car.

As we approached the car from about twenty yards away the trunk looked like it had been opened and then closed, but not closed all the way. My heart started racing as I conjured up images of Donald Bryant freeing himself from the trunk while we had left the car unattended. I imagined him fleeing to a nearby residence or flagging a car down. He would say that he had been kidnapped and forced into the trunk of his own car by a group of robbers and that one of them who goes by Rome killed a man at a convenience store. In addition to all this, Bryant had clearly seen my face. He had sat next to me in the backseat. He could identify me. I would go to prison for the rest of my life for murder. I shared my concerns with K. He too was worried about what would happen if Donald Bryant got away. We couldn't let him go.

When we arrived at the car, I knocked on the trunk nervously. "You still in there?" I asked. "Yeah," he responded. I looked at K. and said, "You know what we gotta do, right?" He nodded. I got in the passenger seat and as K. pulled away, I simply said, "Take me somewhere." What had gotten into me? I didn't even recognize this person. It's like I was in a gangster flick. How quickly my mind had casually decided to murder this man in cold blood. Like I'd done it a hundred times before. In some weird kind of way, it wasn't me anymore. Some other consciousness seemed to have taken over, and I was just watching everything unfold.

I opened another beer and chugged it down. I was already intoxicated, but now the world started spinning. K. saw a cop car and pulled into a secluded spot. I was drunk and needed to throw up. I opened the door and vomited. Then I closed the door, leaned back in my seat, and closed my eyes until I dozed off. I don't know how long I was out before K. woke me up. "We're here," he said. I opened my eyes and had no idea where we were at. Through the windshield I saw waist-high grass and trees in the distance. It felt like we were in the woods. I got out of the car and went to go open the trunk. I didn't want to be the one to do this, but K. never got out of the car. Everything was on me. I had already crossed that line. If I was doomed, why doom K. as well? What difference did it make now? I had already killed one person. My mind fed me every excuse for doing the unthinkable.

I opened the trunk and ordered Donald Bryant to get out. He walked in front of me as I led him about twenty yards into the high grass and pitch-black

THE NEWS & OBSERVER
WEDNESDAY, MAY 25, 1994

METRO

Murderer spared the death penalty

BY SARAH AVERY
STAFF WRITER

RALEIGH — Michael Jerome Braxton's life hung on the votes of two jurors, who held out Tuesday in Wake Superior Court to spare the double murderer the death penalty.

Braxton, 20, was sentenced to two life terms plus 110 years for the Feb 13, 1993, murders of Donald Ray Bryant and Emmanuel Nnji Oguayo.

Braxton will spend at least 60 years in prison Because both murders occurred while he was committing other crimes, he could have been sentenced to die.

"I'm surprised and disappointed," said Colon Willoughby, Wake County district attorney, who prosecuted the case. "For those kinds of brutal crimes, I thought our community would impose the death penalty"

Bryant was shot in the head at close range after being kidnapped and robbed, then forced into the trunk of his car while Braxton and his buddies robbed a Fast Fare on Millbrook Road and killed Oguayo, the store clerk

Jurors split 10-2 in favor of imposing the death penalty in Bryant's murder, with the majority pointing to the brutality of the execution-style slaying.

In the Oguayo slaying, jurors unanimously recommended life imprisonment, having decided that Braxton killed in a moment of panic during the robbery.

"We were 12 honest people with 12 different opinions," jury foreman Jim Appleman said.

Willoughby, whose closing arguments did not explicitly ask jurors to impose the death penalty, chose instead to recite the events the night that Braxton and his buddies set about their spree of violence

Braxton's attorneys, Johnny Gaskins and Andy Gay, worked to show that their client's low self-esteem prompted him to begin drinking at the age of 14, drop out of school and embark on a life of crime.

"Those were compelling issues," Gay said.

Two jurors agreed, according to the foreman Said Appleman: "They were influenced by his background "

For the victim's family as well as Braxton's, the trial's outcome was crushing

"This sends a message to people that you can go ahead and kill somebody and still have your life," said Delores Bryant, who came to the seven-day trial with a photograph of her slain brother pinned to her shirt. "My brother was taken out and slaughtered like an animal."

But Braxton's mother, Marie, wept as her son was sentenced. She testified that he was scarred by a lifetime of social scorn because of his biracial heritage. She is white and Braxton's father is black.

"He is a human being, too," she said after the trial "I know what he did was terrible, and I'm sorry for the families."

News and Observer (Raleigh, NC) article, "Murderer Spared the Death Penalty," May 25, 1994.

darkness. All I could hear was a voice in my head. It was a taunting voice that urged me to kill him. It said, "I don't believe you'll shoot him." Then a hushed whisper: "Pull the trigger, blow his brains out." Then the challenging voice: "You ain't got the heart. I dare you!" Another voice started, "I wonder what . . ." BOOM! I pulled the trigger mid-thought, silencing everything. Before that moment, I still felt like I was watching myself. But when the shot rang out, all the internal voices were silenced, and I was thrust back into my body. I immediately felt a great sense of terror and dread, followed by a sense of utter loneliness. I stepped back, dizzy, and almost fell. Then the intense fear of the consequences of my deeds seized me and I ran out of the darkness toward the glow of the headlights. I got in the car and yelled, "Let's go!"

More than thirty years later, as I admit all this, I'm covered with shame. You can believe yourself to be whatever you want, but it's your decisions that unveil the good and the bad within you. You can think you are in control, but once you embark upon a path of evil, the momentum of your decision-making gains force. You have as much control as a man running down a steep hill. That's why I felt like I was outside of my body, witnessing everything take place. I was witnessing a consciousness born of circumstances I had never before encountered, and I found myself capable of evil I never would have imagined.

Meaner, Angrier, Deadlier

I HAD KILLED TWO PEOPLE during a terrible crime spree. And yet the jury had mercy on me. I was facing the death penalty, and ten of the jurors voted for death, but two voted for life. I was given two life sentences plus 110 years. I was nineteen years old.

In my journey of incarceration, I'd gone from Polk Youth Institution in Raleigh to Southern Correctional Institution in Troy and back to Polk again. From late 1994 to early 1996, I spent twenty months on max lock-up at Blanch Youth Institution near Yanceyville. I was sent there after choking a guard with a belt at Polk on June 19, 1994. I spent my time at Blanch in a cage. Literally a cage. They called it "seg," short for segregation. It's also called "solitary confinement" or "restrictive housing." Same shit, different names.

The cells in seg were tiny. I could extend my arms and touch the walls on both sides with my palms. That's how narrow it was. There was a bunk, a

DC-138
Rev. 11/93

OFFENSE AND DISCIPLINARY REPORT

A. INMATE NAME: Michael Braxton   NCDOC #: 8-7245-544-20673-32

FACILITY: Polk Youth Institution   # 3925   DATE OF REPORT 6-19-94

CRIME ( ) MISD   INMATE ACTIVITY AT   CUSTODY LEVEL AT   DATE OF OFFENSE

CLASS (X) FELON   TIME OF OFFENSE 1   TIME OF OFFENSE Close   06 / 19 / 94

(SEE CODES ON REVERSE SIDE)

I.	II.	III.
A-3	B-8	

OFFENSE CLASS & NUMBER

SUMMARY: On June 19, 1994 Michael Braxton placed a green state issue belt around Officer George neck and began to choke him as he was beening struck.

I hereby waive my right to 24 hours notice before meeting the Hearing Officer.

Inmate's Signature _____   Date: 7-1-94

Is Staff Assistance to the Requested ( ) YES (X) NO. If YES, Staff Assigned _____

My rights with regard to the Disciplinary hearing and review have been explained to me and I hereby acknowledge receipt of these charges.

Inmate's Signature _____   Date / Time: 7-1-94 2:30pm

B. SUPERINTENDENT'S DECISION:

OFFENSE: I. A3   II. 38   III. _____

INMATE PLEA (NG / G* / D): Guilty   Guilty   _____

REFER TO DHO: (Date/Time:) 0   0   _____

Superintendent's Comments: _____

C. HEARING OFFICER'S DECISION:

OFFENSE: I. _____   II. _____   III. _____

INMATE PLEA (NG / G* / D): _____   _____   _____

* PLEA OF GUILTY AND WAIVER OF HEARING

D. PUNISHMENT IMPOSED:

Activate suspended sentence dated_____ for Article(s) _____

(Attach Copy of DC-138)

I. OFFENSE CLASS & NUMBER: A3	II. OFFENSE CLASS & NUMBER: B8	III. OFFENSE CLASS & NUMBER:
30 Days Segregation—Suspend____Months	20 Days Segregation—Suspend____Months	____Days Segregation—Suspend____Months
30 Days Good Time Loss—Suspend____Months	20 Days Good Time Loss—Suspend____Months	____Days Good Time Loss—Suspend____Months
40 Hours Extra Duty—Suspend____Months	30 Hours Extra Duty—Suspend____Months	____Hours Extra Duty—Suspend____Months
Suspension of _____ Privilege(s) for ____Months	Suspension of _____ Privilege(s) for ____Months	Suspension of _____ Privilege(s) for ____Months
Demote to: ( ) Level I	Demote to: ( ) Level I	Demote to: ( ) Level I
Demote to: ( ) Level II	Demote to: ( ) Level II	Demote to: ( ) Level II
Demote to: ( ) Medium	Demote to: ( ) Medium	Demote to: ( ) Medium
Suspended ____Months	Suspended ____Months	Suspended ____Months

_____   7-1-94 7:30pm
Hearing Officer / Superintendent's Signature   Date / time

Distribution: Original (white)—Combined Records; Green—Inmate; Canary—Unit Jacket; Pink—Facility Files; Goldenrod—Inmate

Offense and Disciplinary Report filed after
Braxton assaulted a prison guard at Polk Youth
Institution on June 19, 1994.

toilet, and a sink. That's it. Roaches were everywhere. One morning I woke up to find a rat on my face. I didn't know what it was. I still had my eyes closed when I reached up to brush it away. It then ran across my face, down my chest and under the covers. I jumped straight up from the bed to the toilet. The guards eventually came and killed it. That fucked me up, I ain't gonna lie.

Another thing that fucked me up while I was at Blanch was seeing the COs "using force" on somebody. It was just an opportunity to beat people up. Sometimes I would hear two COs talking, and then one of them might get excited and say he's gonna "take the shield." That's how the COs would enter a cell—in full riot gear with a shield in front of them. For instance, someone might start kicking on their cell door. The CO would come around and give him a "direct order" to stop. If he refused, they would spray him with pepper spray. The COs would then suit up in riot gear, return with the shield, and order the man to hold his hands out through the bars or the trap door to be handcuffed. Whether he obeyed or not, the COs would open the door and fuck him up. They'd beat him with their batons, they'd ram his head into the walls, they'd punch him in the face. Sometimes they did it where nobody could see. Other times they'd beat a man in the middle of the hall where everyone could see. That shit traumatized me.

Another thing that sticks out in my mind from Blanch is that every time I exited my cell I was in full restraint. That meant handcuffs connected to a chain wrapped around my waist and shackles on my ankles, which they called leg irons. Even the few times that my family came to visit, I would be in full restraint even though we were separated by a plexiglass window covered with metal grate. It made me feel like an animal, and I had no human contact for fifteen months. This was part of my punishment for assaulting that CO at Polk.

If that was supposed to break me, they were sorely wrong. All it did was make me meaner, angrier, and deadlier as my heart began to burn with an intense hatred. Being locked in that cell every day made me tougher because I realized that I could endure something I never would've imagined. When they first told me I would do at least two years in seg, I went back to my cell and cried because I didn't think I could make it. But then I adapted and fell into a routine. If this was all they had, they could never break me. At the same time, I soaked up all the barbaric shit I witnessed up close and personal. And then I went somewhere worse.

Orientation at Caledonia

I **HAD HEARD LEGENDS ABOUT** Caledonia State Prison Farm. Old heads
who had been there back in the day talked about how dangerous it was.
I'd heard about stabbings and killings and rape. One of the more popular
stories I'd heard was about a beheading. It was said that one convict killed a
snitch and cut off his head and put it on the warden's desk. They said Caledonia was so big that you could enter with another person and never see him
again for six months. So big that if you tried to escape, you could run for two
days and still be on Caledonia Farm. And Caledonia was a farm—over 7,500
acres. They made you work in the fields just like in the days of slavery. The
guards rode horses and carried shotguns.

All of this was in my head when I arrived at Caledonia in February 1996.
I was twenty-two years old, which meant it was time for me to be transferred
to an adult prison. And because I was in seg at Blanch, I was assigned to
Caledonia because it was one of the few North Carolina prisons at the time
that housed people on I-Con, or Intensive Control, reserved for disruptive

inmates. This was the big league. There were fights and assaults at Blanch, but to my knowledge, nobody had ever been stabbed. And now here I was at Caledonia. I was being transferred with three of my friends—Supreme, Zakil, and TC—but they were assigned to B-Block. I was assigned to E-Block. Which meant I was about to face Caledonia all by myself.

I didn't know what to expect as I was escorted to my cell. I saw figures standing behind their doors, sizing me up as I shuffled to my cell, and when the doors closed behind me, I took a deep breath and realized that this was my life. I ain't never getting out of here, I thought, and I got to do what I got to do to survive.

Because I was on I-Con, I was in my cell for twenty-three hours a day. I couldn't see anything or go out and meet anyone. All I could do was listen. The block was loud. People were yelling to each other from behind their doors. I didn't know what anyone looked like, but before long I had a basic idea of who was who and their relative status based on how they talked and how others talked to them. One name that stuck out in my mind was Trouble.

Just from listening, Trouble sounded like the baddest guy on the block. I learned that he was on lock-up for stabbing someone, and it seemed like he was planning on stabbing somebody else. He talked about the "boys" he was gonna "turn out" and force to become his "punks"—sex slaves. He talked about money and drugs and gambling. All of it seemed to come back to how he was gonna stab this muthafucka if he didn't have his money, or that muthafucka if he shitted him out of some drugs. I just soaked it all up and said in my mind that if this dude even acts like he's coming at me I'm gonna have to kill him. This is how I was mentally preparing myself for life at Caledonia Farm.

The next morning the guards came around and asked me did I want to go outside for recreation. I didn't want to give the appearance that I was afraid to come out of my cell, so I said yes. They handcuffed me and took me to face the unknown.

It was like stepping out into a small city. The recreation area consisted of two basketball courts separated by a fence and surrounded by smaller fenced areas that we called dog cages. There were about a hundred people outside. I was placed in the big cage with one of the basketball courts. I took everything in quietly and walked slowly around the yard. Most of the guys were playing cards, gambling with people in the dog cages, smoking cigarettes, or talking. I didn't know anyone, but I soon recognized the voice I knew to be Trouble. He was a young guy around my age with long dreadlocks down almost to his waist. He walked over to me and said, "Peace God, where you coming from?" I told him that I'd just shipped in from Blanch and had done about twenty months on max and I-Con. This seemed to immediately garner some respect, so I made sure to underline the fact that I had choked a guard out with a belt and got a street charge for it. He asked me how much time I had. When I told him I had two life sentences plus 110 years, I immediately felt the hierarchy shift. I asked him how much time he had. He said he had thirty years on state, then had to do some federal time. I asked him if he was a Godbody. A Godbody is a member of the Nation of Gods and Earths, also called Five Percenters. They believe in an interpretation of Islam that teaches that the Black man is God and that the name Allah is an acronym—Arm Leg Leg Arm Head, which is the body of God. Trouble said he was, but don't nobody respect that Godbody shit here. He told me straight up that he was "living savage." He said he "fucked with the boys," he got money, and got high. He then warned me that everybody at Caledonia was savage. He told me the first thing I needed to do was to get a banger—a shank. "Niggas ain't fighting on the yard, they puttin' steel in muthafuckas," he explained. That's how stabbings were referred to. This was my orientation.

About two or three weeks later, I met the DCC board (Director's Classification Committee), and they promoted me back to regular population. I remember pushing a cart with my personal property on it while being escorted by an officer. There were people everywhere. It felt like every eye was on me. As I stepped on E-Block, the first thing I noticed was that it was overcrowded. When I was at Polk there were over 700 people when the cap was supposed to be around 340. Caledonia was the same. E-Block was made to house twenty-four people since there were only twenty-four cells. But there were at least twenty-four bunk beds placed in the middle of the block's dayroom, and I was assigned to a top bunk. I didn't like the arrangement at all and was concerned about my personal property. I had three standard shipping bags, mainly my books, photos, letters, and hygiene items, but I knew I couldn't fit it all into the small locker at the end of the bunk.

While I stood there trying to figure out where I would put my stuff, I absorbed every action going on around me. I was hyperaware. The first thing that captured my attention—though I made it a point not to appear as if I noticed—was a guy who had the stereotypical look of the most dangerous man in the room. He was huge. He had his shirt off, and he was talking loud enough for me to hear despite being at the opposite end of the block. I caught a glimpse of his face, and I noticed that he had a glass eye. I heard him say something like, "Bitch, get your motherfuckin' ass over here and light my goddamn cigarette!" I saw a white guy walk over and strike a match and hold it to his cigarette. As the big guy sat down, he told the white guy to "sit on Daddy's lap." The white dude was obviously the man's punk and came over and sat down on his lap. I quickly averted my glance. I had never been around anything like this before and feared that someone might try me like that. All I could think about was Trouble's warning to get me a banger as soon as I hit the yard, and I now understood why. If that guy made a move on me like that, I'd have to kill him. This is what you were supposed to do, this is what was expected, I told myself.

Right about then, a guy I knew from Polk named A.K. walked up to me and said, "What's up, Rome? You just getting here?" I was happy to see a familiar face. I asked him if he had a cell. He did, so I asked if I could put my personal property there for now. He told me I could, then started telling me a bit about the yard. He told me that he ran the canteen on E-Block, and that if I needed anything until I got on my feet that he would hold me down. Let me explain what I'm talking about here. At Caledonia there is a central canteen where everybody goes to buy whatever they need: snacks, cigarettes, etc. But on each block (A-Block, B-Block, C-Block, etc.), there is one prisoner who owns the right to buy items from the central canteen and then resell them at a mark-up, usually on credit. So he might buy a twenty-five-cent snack cake and resell it on the block for thirty-five cents. He might buy a pack of cigarettes for a dollar and sell individual cigarettes for twenty cents apiece.

As we were talking, A.K. pointed to a guy who was on his way to the shower and said, "That dude right there, don't never get in the shower if he's in there. And if he gets in there while you are in there, get out, 'cause he is known for knocking muthafuckas out in the shower and raping them." He went on, "You're gonna see a lot of mufuckas doing the boys now, so don't be surprised." I just nodded my head as he continued to talk.

I noticed the big guy with the glass eye kept looking my way while he was talking to someone in one of the cells. The guy was trying to poke his head out to look in my direction as if the two of them were talking about me. The next thing I knew the guy in the cell yelled out, "Who is that white bitch down there?" I felt my heart drop to the floor. I knew he was talking about me. I had just done twenty months on lock-up with very little exposure to sunlight, so my skin was very light, almost pale. He thought I was a white boy. I tried to act like I didn't hear him, but a few seconds later he called out, "Hey girl, come down here and let me talk to you for a minute." I glanced over and saw the guy with the glass eye laughing. My heart was thumping out of my chest. I had never been so humiliated before in my life. I had to do something. If I ignored him, it would only invite more taunts. People would assume that I was weak and scared, and they would prey on me. I *was* scared, but I couldn't let it show.

Again, the guy in the cell yelled out, "Bitch, I know you hear me talking to you!" I don't know if A.K. heard any of this, but I stopped him midsentence and said, "Pardon self, I got to go handle something." I began walking toward the back of the block. All I could think was, "Well, I'm about to get killed on my first day here." I didn't have a banger and didn't think I could beat the big guy with the glass eye in a fistfight. But I didn't have a choice. I was going to walk up to these guys and just start swinging until it was over. If I survived, I'd get a banger and kill one of them. This is what I thought I had to do. I had to show that I was willing to fight, kill, or die at the slightest provocation. I just couldn't believe that I was in a life-or-death situation in my first fifteen minutes on the block.

As I approached closer, doing my best to wear a face of stone, I heard the guy in the cell call my name. "Rome, is that you?" My stomach knotted. I didn't know who he was or if our knowing each other was a good thing. Without showing any fear I kept approaching, still ready to fight. "Yeah. Who dat?"

I finally saw his face and didn't recognize him until he said, "Nigga, this Scarface, man. From Rocky Mount. We was at Troy together." I didn't show any indication that I was happy to see him. We weren't friends at Troy, we were merely there together. And besides, he had disrespected me in front of the whole block. That had to be straightened out first and foremost. I said, "Yeah man, but what's up with this 'white bitch' shit?" He immediately changed his whole tune. He said, "Naw, my nigga, I ain't mean no disrespect. I ain't know that was you. You done get light as a mufucka. What, you just gettin' off lock-up or something?" I told him that I had. He continued, "Yeah, I heard about that shit you did at Polk. They said you wrapped a belt around dude's neck. You crazy as hell, man!" I just nodded and let him talk. He started recounting other events from Troy. He was slightly exaggerating, but I didn't correct him. He was running down my pedigree and establishing my reputation for all who were in earshot, including the guy with the glass eye. Then he started telling me about some of his exploits, including the fact that he "fucked with boys now." I was noticing that this was something that guys took pride in. It was like their way of saying that they had officially graduated from youth spread to adult prison. There was some type of status connected with having a "boy." A sense of power. They bossed the boy around, made him do laundry and run errands, and of course used him for sex. Scarface was proud of this. I didn't express an opinion. It was clear to me that Scarface's position was the consensus way of thinking, and I didn't want to overtly oppose the status quo. After listening to him for a while I started feeling the tension ease, and I told him I had to go unpack.

When I found A.K. to put my property in his cell, I asked him who else was here that was with us at Polk. He said Apple was on B-Block. Me and Apple had become tight at Polk. This kid was only eighteen years old, and he was at Caledonia because he had given the cops a fake birthdate when he was arrested. He was from New York and had more heart than most people I'd ever met. A.K. helped me find him on the yard, and once we greeted each other and dapped it up, I asked him if he had a banger. "No doubt," he said. I told him I needed one bad and he said he'd find me one. In the meantime, I had to get a cell. I couldn't handle sleeping on a bunk in the dayroom after being in segregation for almost two years. I was way too paranoid for that. Apple told me that I had to get a job because all the cells were reserved for workers. "Just tell the sergeant tomorrow that you want a job and they'll put you in the field and give you a cell." I said, "Bet," and I did just that the following day. I didn't get no sleep that night. Just laid awake all night, on edge. The next day I was given a job in the field and moved to A-Block, cell twenty-three.

From the first day I arrived at Caledonia, the seed was planted in my mind that I had to get a banger. That people don't do no fighting here. They put steel in you. This is what was expected of me. I had to prove that if you challenged me, threatened me, or made me feel unsafe, I would kill you. Those who didn't prove themselves became prey. They were the ones who got stabbed, knocked out in the shower and raped, or became boys and lit cigarettes and sat in laps. It was all about self-preservation. I had two life sentences plus 110 years. I was never getting out. That meant I had to be willing to do what was necessary to protect myself for a lifetime.

Convict Carnival

THE YARD AT CALEDONIA was like a convict carnival. Mind you, I was only twenty-two, and Apple—who I knew from Polk and who shouldn't even have been at Caledonia—was eighteen. We were surrounded by men in their thirties, forties, and fifties. Many of them had been in prison for decades. You could tell by the way they dressed and by their sense of style and slang. Some of them wore their pants creased with a tighter fit and tapered at the ankle while most of the younger guys wore baggy pants with no crease and loose legs. It was funny to see some of the older guys with their collars turned up like the Fonz on *Happy Days* and tight t-shirts rolled up above the bicep to show off their muscles.

Everywhere I turned I saw stuff that was shocking to my senses. There were punks with makeup on. Some of them were prostitutes walking the yard advertising themselves. Others were in relationships or had been "turned out" by fear or force. I'd see guys holding hands with them or tongue-kissing and grinding against the walls. I wasn't accustomed to anything like this. On the streets it was taboo. But in Caledonia it was the norm, and nobody gave it a second glance, including the guards.

People were selling weed in nickel bags and trey bags that cost five dollars or three dollars. Others were selling meds: Benadryl (B), Kemadrin (K), and Drixoral (Drix) were the main drugs. There was also homemade wine, called buck, that people sold in Ziploc bags equivalent to a sixteen-ounce cup for one dollar each.

Then there was gambling. You'd walk by and hear somebody advertising, "Chug-a-lug, chug-a lug, chug-a-lug, try your luck, step right up." There was a version of three-card monte going on, and some type of horse race that they played with cards. There were other card games, too—poker, lowball, and Georgia Skin. There were also betting pools on basketball games and NASCAR races. There was constant activity with money being exchanged. I remember looking at the Georgia Skin game and seeing dollars and quarters being bet on the table in plain sight.

The prisoners were in charge of everything. The guards didn't say a word. They were just there to keep you from escaping. In fact, when I talked to my case manager after I'd been there only a couple of days, he asked me straight up, "Do you have a shank?" I said no, of course I didn't. "Well, you might want to get one," he said. I swear by Allah! I couldn't believe it. I didn't know if he was trying to scare me or what, but it branded a mark on my mind. I have to emphasize that I had had almost no human contact for twenty months. I was already paranoid and uneasy around other people. Add this to the fact I was in the most notorious prison in the state and everybody was telling me that I needed a banger.

While I was on A-Block, Apple introduced me to a crew of guys from New York led by Big O. These guys were selling weed, and Big O also controlled the Georgia Skin card game on the yard. A single person would "own" a particular enterprise. Once you owned it, anybody who wanted to play could only play in your game and had to pay you a cut on every deal. I don't know why it was like this, who started it, or how long it had existed, but that's the way it was. Ownership could be transferred only by the owner either giving the rights to someone else or selling it.

Big O and his crew consisted of Supreme, Buddha, Lord, Big Frank, and Apple. Because me and Apple were so close, I was considered "fam." There was another guy on A-Block named Big Duke. He was cool with the crew, but independent. One day he asked me if I wanted to go in on a quarter-ounce of weed—it cost $150, so I would need $75. I only had $20 in my account. So he told me that I could double my money by renting the canteen from Gus, a guy in his late forties who owned the canteen but who never had any money to stock it. He had two life sentences and didn't have any support from the outside, plus he liked to get high. Big Duke said that Gus would let me rent the canteen if I stocked it and gave him a percentage of the profit.

I offered Gus 20 percent of the profit and he agreed. I went to the canteen and spent my twenty dollars and let Gus run it and collect the money. I paid him his cut, reinvested the rest, and after a couple of weeks had enough to go in with Big Duke on a quarter-ounce. What I didn't know until much later was that Big O had been stocking the canteen before I started renting it from Gus, and Big Duke knew it. So I had been stepping on Big O's toes by renting the canteen from Gus. I was as green as a blade of grass and I couldn't see what was going on.

One day on the block there was a huge skirmish. This guy Tony, who owned the lowball game, was playing Scrabble with this white guy named Mike when Lord (one of the guys from Big O's crew) walked up behind Tony and tried to put him in the yoke, a chokehold. Mike jumped up to help him and Apple hit Mike with a chair. Then Big O, Supreme, and Buddha jumped in. They were trying to rob Tony because Big O had just lost $150 to Tony earlier that day on a basketball bet. They were beating his ass and I heard Big O tell Apple to get the banger. I knew that if Apple got the banger, he would stab Tony. Even though I had nothing to do with this, I didn't want Apple to throw his life away by killing Tony for a bet that he had nothing to do with. Apple only had a fourteen-year sentence. Big O had life. I jumped up and ran over to Apple and told him to give me the knife. He tried to tell me to get out of the way, but I refused. I told him straight up: "I ain't gonna let you kill this nigga over somebody else's beef. If Big O wants to kill him, then that's his beef. But you gonna give me that banger!" He gave me the banger, and I'd like to think that I saved his life. Apple is home now. He got out around 2000 or so. We're still friends till this day.

But due to that situation Big O, Supreme, Buddha, Lord, and Apple all got shipped out of the block within three or four days. There was nobody left from their crew except Big Frank and me. So Supreme asked me how much I had. I had about seven dollars. He asked me if Gus had any cigarettes in the canteen. I told him yeah. He said, "Give me all the cigarettes and that seven dollars and you can have half of the Skin game. The other half belongs to Big Frank." I said okay, and like that, I became part owner of one of the most profitable gambling operations at Caledonia.

Big Frank was a Jehovah's Witness. He didn't even cuss, and he wanted no part of the Skin game. So it was all mine, and I didn't even know how to run it, or even how to play it. But I learned. All I had to do, I was told, is buy two decks of cards, one red and one blue. Take a sheet and go outside to the concrete picnic table and lay it on top. Bring about five dollars in quarters because people are going to need change for a dollar. And then just call out, "Georgia Skin!" The players will come. You don't have to play. Just collect fifty cents after every deal.

It seemed simple, but there were a whole lot of people that didn't approve of me owning the game. I was only twenty-two. I had been there no more than two or three months. I had never even played Georgia Skin. Nobody knew who I was. There were people who had been at Caledonia ten to fifteen years who felt that they were entitled to own the game. But I didn't know none of this. For the first three days I would go outside, lay down my sheet, and announce, "Georgia Skin!" But people would just walk right on by me. I was ready to throw in the towel, but Jimmy, the old man who taught me how to run the game, told me not to give up. They were just mad because I owned the game, but they would come because they loved Skinning too much. And he was right. They did come. I carried my banger outside every day at first because I feared that someone was going to try to start their own Skin Game, but nothing like that happened. They were disgruntled, but they started showing up one or two at a time, and before long the game was running at full speed.

After a few weeks the game was running smoothly, so I made a move to buy the card games on A-Block for fifty-five dollars. A few days after that I convinced Gus to sell me ownership of the canteen for thirty dollars. As an incentive I told him I would continue to allow him to operate it for 20 percent of the profit. I was buying up real estate at Caledonia, and people were taking notice. Right after I bought the canteen from Gus, a day or two later, this guy named Everlast approached me in the hall and asked, "Did you buy the canteen from Gus?" I told him yeah, and he said, "That's fucked up. I was trying to buy the canteen. You already own the Skin game and the card games on A-Block." I didn't know what to say. I didn't feel like I had done anything wrong. I was just stupid and thinking I was being a "businessman," but that's how the Shaitan—the devil—tricks you once you are on his path. He's the one guiding you into mischief and evil while you are thinking that you are outsmarting or outmaneuvering everyone else.

Two Codes

THERE ARE TWO CODES I used to live by: the Convict Code and the Code of the Streets. Both are rules that set the standard for acceptable behavior. I invested so much of my life into living by them, only to realize that it was all a sham. None of it was real. All the promises were false. It's like being in a cult. A member of a cult is a true believer, willing to do almost anything for people who are just manipulating them for personal gain. When someone in a cult realizes the truth, it's devastating. It's crushing. But even when they realize the truth and hate the cult, they still can't help but feel some lingering love for the ideal of what they thought life could be. That's why I would say I have a love-hate relationship with the Code of the Streets and the Convict Code.

What used to be referred to as gangsta rap is sometimes just propaganda for "that life," for those codes that romanticize the streets and prison. I loved the music, and so many of the songs are dope. But instead of just enjoying the music, I believed it. I wanted to embody it. Every time a song played, I got to be that person for three to four minutes. It's intoxicating, but it is not real life. It's just an image of a lifestyle, and I bought in to it. I lived it 100 percent. Then I woke up one day and realized that it wasn't real. I was the only one in my circle who fully believed it. I was the only one who was actually putting it into practice. That's how I ended up becoming like a disgruntled soldier. That patriotic soldier who signed up for the military and is ready to put his blood on the line for the principles that he holds dear. He salutes his superiors with respect and will jump on a grenade to serve his nation. He goes to war. He fights. He kills. He suffers. Then one day he finds out that the commander in chief doesn't adhere to the same principles, and neither does the general or the sergeant. And he realizes, just like the cult member, just like the street soldier, that he has been duped by people who never even believed in the rules. Who never accepted the code. They just used it and used me to get ahead. For a long time, it left me feeling bitter and betrayed by aspects of the music that I believed in and loved so much.

So this is deeply personal. I sacrificed my life for a code that was not only immoral but that nobody else in my circle truly adhered to. It angers me. It angers me when I hear other people profess to be a part of that life because I *know* it's mostly just talk. I don't know this from theory, I know it from experience. I can hear them talking about "what needs to be done" or "how we are supposed to carry it." And it's a bunch of tough talk and posturing in front of their peers. Yet there's somebody, just like the kid I used to be, who is gonna hear it and believe it and live that life. That's the same way I feel about "gangsta rap." Some kid like I was is gonna buy in to the propaganda and walk a path that leads to ruin.

Owning the Canteen

THOUGHT I WAS A HUSTLER. You couldn't tell me nothing. I was building a small empire at one of the most notorious prisons in the state, and I was twenty-two years old. It's like I said: when you choose evil, you might think you are in control, but it's like running down a steep hill. You may have taken the first step, but before you know it, gravity takes control, and you go in the direction that the hill wants you to fall. That's basically what happened to me.

One night I was playing cards on A-Block. I was wearing boxers, my shower slippers, and a t-shirt. At 9:45 p.m. the guards would close all the cell doors until shift change at 10 p.m., so you couldn't get in or out of your cell for fifteen minutes. It was during that fifteen-minute interval that I had to use the bathroom. I told Gus to run the game for me while I was gone.

While I was in the bathroom, just an empty cell left open for the guys who slept in the dayroom, three guys walked in. It was Everlast, a guy named Duke (not Big Duke, who had shipped out), and another guy named Prince. I knew something was up, so I turned around to face them. Prince was standing with his hand up under his shirt like he was holding a knife. Everlast and Duke were standing on each side of him. I was surrounded. I said, "What's up?"

Prince said, "I heard you bought the canteen from Gus. That's fucked up." He gestured to Everlast. "My man was supposed to buy the canteen and he been wanting it for a minute. So I'm gonna tell you what you need to do. You need to sell the canteen back to Gus because my man wants it, and what my man wants he gonna get." I sized up the situation and realized that I didn't have a winner. It was three on one, and Prince was acting like he had a knife. "Gus was supposed to sell you the canteen?" I asked. Everlast nodded. So I said, "Man, that's fucked up. He ain't tell me that shit. I'm gonna go get him right now and we gonna straighten this situation out. If he was supposed to sell you the canteen and he put me in the middle of this, then I'm gonna slap the shit out of him and sell you the canteen. Matter fact, let me go get him." And I walked out.

I had no real intention of doing any of that, but I had to get out of that bathroom. I walked down to where Gus was running the card game and pulled him aside. I told him, "Look, Everlast and Prince and them just stepped to me in the bathroom and told me that you was supposed to sell them the canteen, and they telling me I need to sell it back to you so they can buy it." Gus said, "Man, fuck them niggas, Rome. That was my canteen, and I can sell it to whoever I want to. You ain't got to sell shit." I told him I wasn't intending on doing any of that, I just needed to make it look like we were talking about it until they opened the cell doors at 10 p.m. and I could go to my cell, put on my pants and boots, and get my banger. Gus tried to brush it off like none of that was necessary, but he didn't understand how they had approached me. I couldn't let this ride. If I did, I would be inviting more trouble. Even if it wasn't from them. Word would get out that three dudes had stepped to me in the bathroom and I didn't do nothing. It would only embolden someone else to do the same thing. But next time somebody might actually attack me. I had to respond.

When 10 p.m. arrived, I went in my cell, put on my pants and boots, and got my banger. I always kept it in a pair of construction gloves that I used when I worked in the fields. I could slide it down into one of the fingers and just a bit of the handle would be sticking out. I'd take the work gloves with the shank in them and put them in my back pocket with the fingers facing up. That way when I walked around it just looked like I had a pair of work gloves in my back pocket, but the banger was easily accessible.

I walked right back to where Prince, Everlast, and Duke were standing. My adrenaline was surging. I figured I might get stabbed or killed, but one of these guys was gonna die with me. I was coming to kill. I refused to leave an injured enemy who might kill me one day in retaliation. I said, "Now, what was y'all saying about the canteen?" I swear by Allah all three of them were silent. I was emboldened by their silence. I looked at Prince and said, "I thought you said what your man wants he gonna get." Prince nodded his head slowly but didn't say a word. I walked over to Everlast and said, "Well, what you want, bruh?" He didn't say nothing, didn't even raise his eyes to meet mine. I was waiting for anything to trigger me, but there was nothing. My heart was racing, but I said in a loud voice: "I'll tell you muthafuckas what, I'm getting ready to go down here and play some cards. And tomorrow I'm gonna stock the canteen, and if any one of you want something you best bring your money 'cause I'm through with this talk about who owns the canteen." And I walked off and went to play cards.

I played two hands but couldn't focus—the tension was too thick. So I shut the game down, took my chair and sat with my back to the wall so I could see everything. I just waited and stewed.

Big Frank came and sat beside me and asked me what was going on. I told him nothing. He said he could sense that something was wrong. As we were sitting there, Duke walked up to Big Frank and asked to have a word with him. The two of them walked off together and after five minutes or so Big Frank came back with a message. "Them guys said they want to squash that whole thing about the canteen." I said, "It's too late for that." He said, "Why is it too late?" I said, "Because they stepped to me trying to put some muscle down, and this nigga Prince acting like he got a banger under his shirt." Big Frank asked, "Well, what you gonna do?" I said I'm just gonna bide my time and catch Prince on the one-on-one, and then I'm gonna stab him. He said, "Naw, Rome you ain't gotta do that. Them niggas don't want no beef like that." I said, "Well they should've thought about that before they stepped to me in the bathroom. I gotta straighten that shit." Big Frank said, "But why you feel like you gotta stab 'em? Why don't you just beat his tail or something?" I said, "Because that nigga might have a banger. I ain't trying to run up on nobody for no fistfight and he got a banger." Big Frank said, "Well, why don't you catch him somewhere that you know he won't have a banger?" "Like where?" I asked. He said "At the chow hall. Just beat his tail, Rome. I promise you none of them jokers want more than that." I thought about what he said and finally agreed.

The next morning, we went to breakfast around 7 a.m. I made sure to be the last person coming in the chow hall so Prince would be there before me. As soon as I walked in, I saw he was by himself. I walked right up to him and said, "You remember how you stepped to me yesterday?" He nodded his head. I said, "Well, don't you ever step to me like that again." Then I slapped him with an open hand. A slap is more disrespectful than a punch and I wanted to disrespect him publicly. A slap is also louder than a punch so everybody would hear it. After I slapped him, he tried to grab me and I threw him on top of a table and then the guards came and broke it up.

They locked me in my cell on A-Block and locked Prince up elsewhere. Maybe thirty minutes later Everlast came to my cell door and said, "That's fucked up. We thought that shit was squashed. But we gonna get your ass when you get off lock-up." I didn't say a word as he walked off huffing and puffing.

Two days later an officer escorted me from my cell to the unit manager's office. He told me I was charged with fighting in the chow hall and if I wanted to plead guilty, he'd let me off lock-up with reduced punishment. So I pleaded guilty. Then he told me to sign a piece of paper that said I wasn't in fear for my life and that I was returning to regular population of my own free will. It was a form that freed the prison of any responsibility if I got killed after returning to the yard from a fight. I signed the paper and was free to go.

I went back to my cell and got my banger and put on my winter coat to protect me from being seriously wounded if I got stabbed. I went to the yard to wait for Prince and Everlast. I had my shades on and a black bandanna. I stood in a corner of the yard where I could watch the door and see everyone who came outside. Finally, I saw Prince, Everlast, and Duke. They came outside and stood across the yard from me. I waited. I felt like the onus was on them. I didn't have anything to straighten. I had slapped him. If he felt like he needed to straighten it, then he had to bring it to me. So I waited and waited in the hot sun, sweating in my winter coat.

After about thirty minutes this guy named Brown Eyes walked up to me and fired up a blunt and passed it to me. After we finished smoking, I was so high I felt like I was gonna faint in the heat. I could barely maintain my composure as I walked back to my cell, fearing that the guys were gonna make a move on me and I wouldn't be able to defend myself. Once I made it to my cell I closed my door, took off the coat, and went to sleep. A week later Prince moved back on to A-Block and I was constantly paranoid that he, Everlast, and Duke were going to try and catch me and stab me.

The Bible Don't Say Nothing about Pork

MY MOTHER WASN'T OVERTLY RELIGIOUS, but she did teach me the basic tenets of the Christian faith. I never had a reason to question my beliefs. Mama taught me about Jesus, and although I'd never read the Bible, I believed it was the absolute word of God. We get our religion from our parents, and we don't often do any independent study of our own. In fact, Prophet Muhammad (may the peace and blessings of Allah be upon him) said that all children are born with the disposition to acknowledge and worship One God, but it is their parents who make them a Jew, a Christian, or a Muslim. As we grow, we often develop a sense of moral duty to adhere to the beliefs of our parents. This is among the main hindrances preventing people from exploring a religion other than their own. I imagine the same might have been true for me if someone had tried to introduce me to Islam when I was younger. I would've looked at it as something foreign, and I likely would've rejected it. But Allah guided me through a different way.

When I arrived at Caledonia in 1996, I was still on my long journey to becoming the Muslim I am today. But let me back up a few years to give you a sense of that journey. In 1991, I was serving time for several misdemeanor convictions at Triangle Correctional in Raleigh. One Saturday morning I was on my bunk in a dorm of about forty to fifty people. A small group gathered around the bunk next to mine listening to a man preach from the Book of Revelation about the mark of the beast. I found myself listening, too. He proclaimed that America was the prophesied "Mystery Babylon" and that she was corrupt and filled with sin. He said that among her greatest sins was that she had enslaved and deceived the people of God—Black people. He talked about the coming of the New World Order and how money was going to become obsolete. Anyone who wanted to buy or sell would have to get a computer strip beneath the skin of their hand, which he said was the mark of the beast.

All this was fascinating to my eighteen-year-old mind. It all seemed to be written right there in the Bible, a book I believed was the word of God. So after his sermon I decided to talk to this man, who had taken on Reuben as his righteous name. He explained that he was a Hebrew Israelite. When I asked him what that was, he said it was the true nationality and identity of the Black race in America. He said that this was the world's best-kept secret. He showed me several passages in the Bible that he said proved his claim. "My people are destroyed because of a lack of knowledge," he quoted. This meant that the Black nation had been destroyed because they lacked the knowledge of self and God, he explained. All our problems were linked back to slavery, when we were systematically stripped of the true knowledge of self, and because we didn't know our God we didn't know how to call on Him.

He explained that Abraham was a Hebrew (Genesis 14:13) and that his grandson Jacob was named Israel by the angel of God. He pointed to a passage (Genesis 15:13–14) where God said to Abraham to "know of a surety that your seed shall be a stranger in the land that is not theirs and they shall serve them and be afflicted for four hundred years." He said that this was proof of our identity. That Black people in America were the only people in the world who had been enslaved in a land that was not theirs for four hundred years. This meant that we were the seed—the descendants—of Abraham and Jacob, thus making Hebrew Israelite our true identity.

This was mind-blowing stuff. I couldn't believe that the Bible held such secrets about race and identity. After that, I started reading the Bible every day and hanging around Reuben. I was like a sponge trying to soak up everything he knew. One day during lunchtime I went through the line and got my tray. They were serving barbecue pork that day, and I noticed Reuben sitting alone in the chow hall, so I walked over to join him. As soon as I sat down, he said "Shalom," and got his stuff and left. I felt slighted and a little foolish, like he had just dissed me. Maybe I was annoying him—after all, I was eighteen and he was in his thirties. I decided to approach him about it after lunch.

As soon as I saw him on the yard, I stepped to him and asked if I was getting on his nerves or playing him too close. He looked confused and asked me why I would think that. I mentioned how he'd abruptly left the table when I sat down at the chow hall and he said, "Naw, brother, you had pork on your tray. I don't eat pork and didn't want to be in your presence while you were eating it." I figured he must have some type of medical condition, so I asked, "What's wrong with you? You allergic to pork or something?" He laughed and said, "Naw, brother, God forbade it."

"Where you get that from?" I asked.

"It's written in the Bible."

He said he'd show me, and we headed to the dorm to get our bibles. I had this nervous feeling along the way. I feared that I was gonna lose confidence in what he said because I was almost 100 percent sure that the Bible didn't say, "Thou shalt not eat pork." I knew it couldn't be true because I'd eaten pork practically every day for as long as I could remember. It was bacon, sausage, or country ham for breakfast, barbecue or pot roast or neck bones for lunch, pork chop or ribs for dinner. Everybody I knew ate pork. Hell, even the preachers and all the people at church ate pork. I'd been to pig pickings. I couldn't imagine how a person was supposed to survive without eating pork. Plus, I wondered why God would forbid it. It was just food.

When we got back to the dorm, he instructed me to turn to Leviticus 11 and read up to verse 8. I did, then I turned to him and said, "I don't get it. It says not to eat the camel, the coney, the hare, and the swine. It don't say nothing about pork." He looked at me, and I imagine he had to be holding back a smile at my ignorance, but he just asked, "Do you know what swine is?" I told him I didn't. He told me to go to the prison library and look it up.

I rushed back to the dorm to tell Reuben. "You were right! The Bible says not to eat pork!" I asked him how come other people didn't know this, and he told me something that would guide me from that day forward on to the path of knowledge: "Brother, if you ever want to hide something from a nigger, put it in a book." There was an entire world of secrets and knowledge out there waiting for me to discover, and I was determined that no one would keep me ignorant. When I got out, I was going to go to the library and order the biggest book they had. I was now on the path of knowledge.

For about three months during that time in prison I became a Black Hebrew Israelite. This was my first introduction to any tradition outside of Christianity. I took on my first religious name, Mikhail Yeshua Yisraeli, which I kept for a few years. Matter of fact, there are still people who know me as Mikhail.

Reuben left me with this verse from the Book of Proverbs as a guide: "Knowledge is the principal thing. Therefore, get knowledge. But with all thine getting, get understanding." Alhamdulillah! That was over thirty years ago, and Allah has guided me through the Hebrew Israelites, the Five Percenters, and the Nation of Islam to the message that He revealed to Prophet Muhammad (peace and blessings be upon him) and the Holy Qur'an, and it was through the acquisition of knowledge and understanding.

Does my faith influence my identity as an MC? Has it shaped my rhymes? Absolutely. But a lot of my rhymes predate my practice of Islam. I have a lot of dark, depressing content, and I've struggled with whether I should release these songs. But I need to include them to fully show my growth. Today, everything I write connects to my identity as a Muslim because I fear Allah and my conscience guides me in what I write. I'm responsible and accountable for what I do and say and therefore I fear displeasing my Lord and influencing someone with lyrics that could encourage the type of behavior that I oppose. I believe that my music is a form of *dawah*. In Arabic that means "to invite," and it is synonymous with propagating the faith. For me, as an MC, my lyrics are dawah. It's my way of saying: listen to my story. See where I've come from and where I am today and how I arrived here. Throughout history, culture has been spread through the arts, and this is my vision for ultimately introducing my faith through the art of lyricism and storytelling. I have a name for it. It's called Hip Haqq. *Haqq* is an Arabic word that means "truth." I want to make the truth sound hip and attractive and turn people to what is good and away from the type of message in music that promotes violence, misogyny, and drugs. That's really what I'm striving for, to do something good with the abilities Allah has given me before I leave this earth.

Slave Labor

CALEDONIA WAS A WORK FARM, and if you had a cell, then you had to work out in the field. Growing up, I'd never done any real hard labor. I had a few fast-food jobs, I did a little construction work with my dad, and I had a paper route. But I'd never done much labor out in the sun except for mowing the lawn. At Caledonia, it was real sweat-of-the-brow prison labor.

Every Monday through Friday morning, right after breakfast, all the workers had to report to the front yard. The yard was surrounded by a fence, and there was a secure entrance, called a sally port, where the bus would pull in. A guard would get out of the bus and unlock the gate while the driver drove into the sally port. Then he'd lock the gate and unlock another gate for us to get on the bus. The guard would do a roll call, and about twenty-five of us would climb onto the bus through the back door. There was a steel barrier and a thick metal screen separating the guards from the passengers. There would usually be about three or four buses going out every day with a squad of workers. One squad might work potatoes, another pick squash, another pick cucumbers, and another cabbage. I picked all those as well as tomatoes, watermelon, cantaloupes, and sweet potatoes.

When we arrived at a plot, the guards would get out, and two or three would mount horses. Once the officers were on horseback, they'd ride off a ways, and then another guard would come and unlock the back door to let us out. This guard was known as the foreman or the groundsman. The guards on horseback carried shotguns and pistols, but the foreman had no weapons. The two or three horsemen would get in formation with one as the lead and the other the tail. Say our squad was working on potatoes. We might do four rows at a time. The lead horse would be fifty yards ahead and two or three rows to our side. As we worked down the row we could only go as far as being parallel to the lead horse, and the tail horse would follow about fifteen yards behind us. Once everybody caught up to the lead horse, he'd trot out another fifty yards and we'd start working until we were parallel again. The foreman would be on the ground supervising. I used to wonder if this was how my ancestors felt out there in the hot sun, with white men on horseback wearing cowboy hats, chewing tobacco, and carrying shotguns, watching their every move.

I was in prison for life, just like a slave was a slave for life. I had no freedom and no power. I knew, just like my ancestors knew, that if I took off running, I would be killed. It was a feeling of being completely dominated. I was a slave. My family had no rights over me. I was the property of the state of North Carolina. In fact, people used to say all the time that if an inmate got hurt or killed, then the worst thing you could be charged with was damage to state property. Perhaps that was just a legend, but every aspect of Caledonia felt like being on a plantation. In fact, Caledonia was once a massive plantation — hundreds of slaves had worked in these same fields for generations. (In 2021, Caledonia became the Roanoke River Correctional Institution. I guess they stopped taking pride in being named after a slave plantation.)

One day in July 1996, I was out in the field working the sweet potatoes. The foreman told us to pull up all the weeds. I worked busily, snatching up weeds until I had gotten ahead of everyone else and came parallel to the lead horse. I stopped to wait for everybody to catch up. The foreman saw me and began inspecting my row. He claimed that I had missed a lot of weeds and was loafing around. I told him that I had already done my row. He told me to go help do another row, then. I felt like I was being assigned extra work simply because I was quicker than everyone else. If anything, those other guys were loafing. I can't remember exactly what he said but it was aggressive and disrespectful. I lost my cool. I started walking toward him with my fists balled up said, "I'm gonna bust your muthafuckin' ass." A couple of guys held me back, and I heard a shotgun being pumped. The foreman handcuffed me and called for the dog truck.

The dog truck is just what it sounds like, a pickup truck with a built-in dog cage in the cab. It's how they transport the dogs that track escaped prisoners. They put me in the dog cage and the foreman came up and gave me a warning. "Look here, son, I ain't gonna say you won't bust my ass. But you ain't got no win out here, because if you were to even take a swing at me, them officers out there on horseback carrying them shotguns would shoot you, man. So you need to think real hard about that because this ain't no game, son." I didn't respond, but the gravity of everything he said sank in. I had assaulted an officer at Polk and lived to tell about it, but out here, if I even attempted to fight, I could be killed. This is what life in prison felt like. A slave with no power over my own body. The dog truck carried me back to the prison, and I was placed on lock-up. Prison is the modern-day slave plantation. Ain't no way around it, and there ain't nothing just or humane in this shit.

Ready 4 War

They got me locked up
Boxed up
Bound and chained
In a steel cubicle walking around deranged
Pacin' like a caged lion
Handcuffs and leg irons
Chain on my waist
Pain on my face
I keep my brain on my case
But my eyes can't hide the anger
I might murk a cat and hide the banger
Living amongst strangers
Godbodies and Hell's Angels
Armageddon

The drama is settin'
My mama's regretting
She ever had me
Fuck it I'm livin' madly
Haters they wanna bag me
Hungry to stab me
Cops rollin' five deep lustin' to bank me
The bastards hate me
They wanna strap me down and try to sedate me
But lately
I've had flashbacks
Of runaway slaves with lashed backs
Angry harassed Blacks
On top of that
I feel the spirit of the Prophet Nat Turner
On some underground railroad shit, give me a burner
It's Revolution!
Burn the flag and piss on the Constitution
I'm Ready 4 War!

Straight revolutionary state of mind right here when I wrote this in 2002 or 2003. I was in lock-up at the time. I was channeling that Black slave who was captured in Africa, chained, and held in the hull of a ship for three months or more in his own waste, sores festering on his body. Finally making it to American soil to be held in a jail cell as his injuries healed and he picked up a few pounds. Then he was placed on an auction block for spectators to ogle and examine while he was nude. They inspected his genitals, made him open his mouth, and they checked his teeth. Then he was sold to a slaveowner who took him to a plantation where no one could speak his language, and he was forced to work. He felt the lash on his back from the master's whip. He felt the anger surge within his chest, but he could not act. He suffered. He endured, and slowly, ever so slowly, he was broken. Yet the anger still surged in his heart. I am the descendant of these men, and when I spit these words, I feel an entire legacy of struggle surging through my veins.

I Need a New Shank

THE DAY AFTER I threatened the officer in Caledonia, in July 1996, I was at my cell door looking out the window when I noticed a new guy was moving in to the block. It was my friend Zakil! He was finally getting off I-Con after five months. I was happy to see him, and I immediately banged on my door to get his attention. Now that Apple had shipped out, I wasn't close with anyone and was eager to bond with someone that I had history with prior to Caledonia. So when Zakil came over to my cell door I greeted him like we were long lost friends. I told him that I owned the canteen and the card games and if he needed anything to just let me know. He was kind of expressionless, and in retrospect I guess he was acting like I did when I first got to Caledonia: just soaking everything in.

I asked him did he have any cigarettes and he said no. I told him again that if he needed anything I had it. He said he didn't have any money and that it might be another month before he got any. No problem, I told him. I called Gus over to my door and said, "Look, Gus, this is my man Zakil. He just got off lock-up and he ain't got nothing. Anything he wants, you let him get it and just put it on a separate tab. Don't put it on the weekly credit sheet because he'll pay it whenever he can." Gus said okay, and Zakil said thanks and left to go unpack his stuff.

An hour or so later I saw Zakil talking to Prince, Everlast, and Duke. A few moments later Zakil went to Gus and got some cigarettes and snacks from the canteen, and when he returned, he shared them with the three men. Of course, he had no idea about my history with them or that Prince and I had fought. I just shook my head and thought to myself that he was choosing the wrong crowd. Maybe I should've said something to him, but I figured it wouldn't matter. He'd still choose to hang out with them, and sometimes experience is the best teacher. I just never envisioned that things would play out the way they did.

On August 6, 1996, Duke allegedly stole somebody's radio on A-Block. Somebody said they saw Duke go into the guy's cell and steal it and sell it on the yard. Duke was outside while this conversation was taking place on the block, and the next thing I knew, a group of guys packed all of Duke's stuff and set it in the sally port, right at the entrance door. They had decided that Duke had to move. If he tried to come back on the block somebody was gonna kill him.

When the yard closed and Duke came back to A-Block, he saw all his stuff packed up by the door. Somebody came up and told him that if he tried to come back on the block it was gonna be a problem. When the guards ordered him to return to his cell block, he refused, and that's when they learned that Duke was being forced off the block. They entered the block about eight to ten deep and made everyone leave. The guards were standing in a line at the entrance and were searching everyone as they left the block. I had my shank on me and I didn't have time to hide it, so I just stepped in my cell and put it up under my mattress and came back out. Then the guards did a complete search of A-Block. When they came out, they had at least fifty shanks. Some of them were huge and looked like machetes. There were lawn mower blades, ice picks, daggers, and knives sharp as razor blades on both sides. When I saw the caliber of weaponry that was up in A-Block alone, I felt embarrassed by my ice pick. It was like having a .25 pistol when everybody else has AK-47s. What was I gonna do with my ice pick if a dude pulled a machete on me?

After the shakedown, I was locked in my cell. They had found the shank I had placed under my mattress. Nobody else got charged with anything because the rest of the shanks were found in public places like the bathroom, the janitor's closet, the lights in the shower, or the ceiling. Two days later the unit manager let me off lock-up. I pleaded guilty to a weapons charge and was sentenced to twenty days of segregation. But I only did two days and was right back on the yard. Now I needed another shank.

It just so happened that within a week of that shakedown somebody on A-Block had stolen a metal file from maintenance and about ten feet of fence posting. This was good metal for making shanks, especially with a metal file. I put in an order from the guy that made them—a white guy. I paid him ten dollars, and he gave me a shank that was razor sharp on the edges, with an arrow-like point. It was flat, about an inch wide and eight to ten inches long. He made a handle for it using the suede leather tongue from a boot tied on in a cross pattern using dental floss. This was heavy artillery, and mine wasn't one-of-a-kind. Several people had bought shanks from him just like that. Nevertheless, I felt more secure with this than I had been before.

Toxic Masculinity

SOMEONE RECENTLY SHARED WITH ME this definition of toxic masculinity: "a narrow and repressive description of manhood, designating manhood as defined by violence, sex, status and aggression." I thought it was spot on. It has been the yardstick by which I've measured my self-worth. In many ways I feel like it still has a hold on me. It's all I've been around and what I'm still around. For instance, violence. I don't like violence now, and I haven't committed an act of violence in well over twenty-five years. But I know that a lot of my status, the respect that I receive, is based on the violence I committed in the past. In prison, I don't know if I could have survived without violence. What I mean is I don't know if I could be the person that I am today had I not established a reputation for violence in the past. Today, if someone offends me, I have the option of letting it slide. I can forgive that person and not lose any respect. People won't look at me as soft, scared, or weak. In fact, they will say, "Alim let that go because he didn't want to kill him." And that's the truth. I don't want to kill anyone. I don't want to hurt anyone. And I'm grateful that I can let things slide if I choose. Had I never established a reputation for violence when I was younger, I could never act the way I do now because people would interpret it as weakness.

The same thing with sex. When I was maybe eleven or twelve, my mom's boyfriend Catbird asked me one day if I'd ever had any pussy. I was embarrassed that he'd asked me something like that in such bold language. I lied and said I had. He asked me if I had a girlfriend and I said I did. A few months later he and I were at the convenience store and a girl around my age came in and I could tell she liked me. Catbird said, "I think that girl likes you. Go talk to her." "But I've got a girlfriend!" I responded. "So what?" he said. "Boy, you don't never turn down no pussy!" After that, I practically lived by that motto to the point that I never had a single girlfriend that I was faithful to. It wasn't until I became Muslim and began to model myself after the morals and virtues of the Prophet Muhammad (may the peace and blessings of Allah be upon him) did I begin to change my conduct and thinking. Now I strongly value the sanctity of marriage and being faithful to my wife. I wish I would've been exposed to such strong values earlier in life, but nonetheless I have a great appreciation for them now.

In prison, toxic masculinity is what everybody expects of you. I'll give you two examples from my experience. "Gunslinging" is penitentiary slang for exposing yourself to a female guard while masturbating. It is such an epidemic that it's considered by most prisoners to be an acceptable practice. This is a testament to the moral decrepitude and complete loss of shame and self-respect that occurs in prison. Literally all day long dudes carry on conversations about gunslinging. There are some who call themselves snipers. They hide in mop closets or lurk behind doors, masturbating while watching a fully clothed woman performing her duties. She may be writing or talking on the phone, the most mundane things. Then there are those who openly expose themselves when a female guard comes by their cell. They may stand in the middle of the floor naked and masturbate so that the guard will see them. It's an almost daily occurrence to hear a female guard rebuking someone who is masturbating.

I encountered gunslinging when I first got to prison at Polk Youth Institution in 1993. I didn't understand it at first. How do you even masturbate to a woman who has on all her clothes? It didn't make sense to me. Just seeing a woman doing her job didn't turn me on. But the thought intrigued me, I'm not gonna lie. Once Shaitan planted the suggestion in my mind I was curious about why this seemed so thrilling.

So one night while I was on my bunk I saw one of the guards was sitting on a stool monitoring the block. I began to masturbate beneath my covers and stare at her. I had never even spoken to this woman, but here I was masturbating and staring boldly at her. She noticed what I was doing and looked away. I took that as approval, or permission, and I stared at her even more intently. She looked again and then caught eye contact with me for a second and again averted her gaze. She seemed to be squirming on the stool and I told myself that she liked it. Then she looked at me again, dead in the eyes, but with a look of annoyance. She crooked her finger, indicating for me to come to her. I felt my heart drop and I quickly tried to make myself presentable as I walked to the bars. She had a very stern look and said, "Do you think I want to see that? Do you think that turns me on? It doesn't. Now put it up and go to sleep." I said, "Yes ma'am," and felt smaller than a grain of rice. I was so humiliated. I went to bed and that was the end of that. I've never tried anything like that again. Although I was embarrassed, I'm glad it happened because it ultimately deterred me from plunging into this toxic behavior.

Here's another example. A few years ago, I was sitting on the block watching a football game when I heard someone holler out, "Goddamn! Oh, shit." I turned around and saw a dude I'll call D and a brother I'll call Akh. I noticed D had blood on the back of his shirt. Akh had a shank in his hand. D grabbed a push broom, swinging it fiercely, then he took the bottom off and wielded it like a bat. Akh backed off and went upstairs to his cell. D's entire shirt was bloody in the back, and blood was dripping down his shorts and boxers and all over the floor. He was still wielding the broom, so I picked up my belongings and went to my cell. I didn't want to be implicated in whatever was going down, and I wasn't going to sit around and get cracked in the head either. I went to my cell and just sat in my chair at the door. Akh and D began to convey threats back and forth to each other. Akh told D he was gonna kill him, and D said to come and get him. D was bleeding bad. I looked around the block to see if anybody was going to intervene, but nobody moved or said a word.

So I made the decision to try and talk Akh out of killing D. If I didn't at least try, I'd feel like I silently condoned it. I went to Akh's cell. He was putting on armor. He had a shield that he had fixed around his arm and a shank in his right hand. I said very cautiously, "Akh, I ain't got nothing to do with this and I don't know what's going on, but I just want you to know that you don't have to kill him." He shook his head, "It's too late." I said, "Naw, it's not too late. He's still alive. And you don't have to kill him." He said again, "It's too late. He got to go." I said, "Brother, you don't want to do this. I don't know what he's done to you but it's not worth throwing away your life. And if you kill this man, you will be throwing away the rest of your life. Trust me, I'm telling you from experience. Whatever he did it's not worth it." He said, "That muthafucka got to go. He cannot stay on the block with me no more. He got to get the fuck out of here." "If that's what you want, *I'll* get him out of here," I told him. "Just don't kill him. Give me a few minutes and I promise I'll get him out of here." Akh seemed to agree but just said, "Get him the fuck out of here."

I rushed downstairs. D was now on the floor and his eyes were rolling back. I got two guys to help me get him up. We lifted him off the ground and set him on his feet. His eyes opened and he asked me, "What's going on?" I said, "You got to go! You need medical help. You're gonna bleed to death." He said, "I need my glasses and my jumpsuit." I ran and got both and helped him get dressed. "What am I supposed to say?" he asked me. "I'm not gonna tell on him." I said, "Man, just go to the nurse and let everything take its course. But you need to go *now*." He said, "Alright, thank you. Listen, I just want you to know I love you." "Just go, man," I said. "Get you some help." And he left.

I live in an environment where caring and compassion are seen as weak and unmanly, where conflict is usually resolved with violence. You feel like violence is what everybody expects of you, that you don't have any other options. This isn't unique to the prison environment, although in prison it finds its fullest expression. A lot of times people don't know what to do in a conflict situation, so they say something extreme like, "I'ma kill that muthafucka" or "I'ma fuck that muthafucka up." I've heard it dozens of times. And if they don't get any pushback like, "Naw, man you ain't got to kill him," or "You ain't got to fuck him up, all you gotta do is . . . ," then they feel like they don't have any options. Silence is akin to approval. In all the conflicts I've resolved over the years I've learned that in almost every case neither party wanted to resort to violence. They just thought it was their only option. But 90 percent of the time, once they are given alternatives, they take the option that doesn't result in violence. It's when people think they have no other options that violence pops off. Where I came from, the way I grew up, you had to be tough, you had to be hard. You had to appear as though you were heartless, and therefore goodness gets suppressed. For me, it got pushed down so deep that even I forgot it was there. Call it toxic masculinity, but it's all I knew.

I've been fortunate, though, to have had my eyes opened to the dangers of toxic masculinity and to the struggles of women. Back in 2014 when I was meeting with a group of volunteers, one of them—Jennifer Thompson—was talking about a new book called *Bad Feminist* by Roxanne Gay. (I later read the book myself.) I don't remember the exact discussion, but I said something that unmasked my ignorance about the experience of women. Jennifer's response was passionate, fiery, and authoritative. I could tell she was furious, but she also spoke to me with great caring. She explained to me what it is like to live in the world as a woman. She talked about feeling vulnerable and unsafe. How she is looked at and spoken to by men she doesn't know when she goes to the gas station or the grocery store. How this makes her feel anxious and afraid. As I listened to her, I began to remember the times I'd been in the "wrong" neighborhood and hardly knew anyone. It would feel like a hundred pairs of menacing eyes staring at me as I walked down the street. I heard disrespectful comments hurled in my direction, but I couldn't respond. I didn't know if someone was going to attack me. It was intimidating and frightening. This is what Jennifer felt. She told me that this is what the women in my life feel—every day. Hearing that was powerful! Hell, I've ogled more than my fair share of women and have undoubtedly said inappropriate things. Never did I imagine that I made them feel unsafe. But, thanks to Jennifer, I started to understand. I regretted my behavior and felt shame for my actions.

That experience would later help me understand the shame and guilt felt by some white people as they start to understand the impact of white privilege and how their behavior may unconsciously contribute to the racism that Black people feel every day. It's weird how one thing can shed light on another, but that's how it is.

I Had to Put Steel in Him

ABOUT A WEEK AFTER the shakedown that led me to lose my first banger, Zakil got locked up for refusing to work. I now know that it was Wednesday, August 14, 1996. He was still on the block, though, just confined to his cell. That same day he had gotten a money order from his family and said he would pay me on Friday, two days later. I said okay and called Gus over to tally his bill. It came to $17.10. This was what he had gotten on credit from my canteen since July 3.

Friday was the day the guards came around to pay out withdrawals from our accounts. After everyone was paid, Gus went around and collected the money we were owed and brought it to me. But Zakil hadn't paid yet. Gus explained that Zakil had given Prince the money to pay me, but that Prince lost it all playing cards. I shook my head and thought to myself, *Now he's finally gonna learn that Prince is bad company.* At Caledonia there were rules when it came to borrowing and loaning money and paying your debts.

For instance, you were supposed to pay your debts before you did anything else because that money no longer belonged to you. It didn't matter if it left you broke. The attitude of the loan shark was: "When you wanted to borrow money, I didn't have to run you down to loan it to you, so I shouldn't have to run you down to get what's mine."

There were all kinds of hustlers and bullshitters at Caledonia. People always had an excuse for why they didn't have your money. I observed how sharks handled these situations differently. Some sharks would verbally chastise borrowers, or sweet-talk them, or act like they were giving them advice. It was a give-and-take situation. The borrower got what he wanted, and the shark got to feel important by humiliating him, grandstanding, or acting like a boss. Others claimed to have zero tolerance, meaning that if you didn't have their money on payday, they were gonna "put that steel in you." But most sharks were open to negotiation. They would listen to your excuses and try to work out a payment plan. They didn't want to stab or kill you—the endgame was to get the money. If they recognized that you were giving them the runaround, they might waive the debt altogether and cut ties with you. The mindset was that it was gonna hurt you more in the long run because you were harming your reputation and wouldn't be able to get nothing from nobody. I'd hear sharks say things like, "It only cost me five dollars to learn not to fuck with him no more. That lesson was real cheap." From these interactions everyone learned who the "pay masters" were—those with solid-gold credit. And everybody learned who the high-risk borrowers were. Whether one was a pay master or a high-risk borrower, there was one universal rule: you never tell a man that he was beat. That was the worst possible thing that could be done in the loan-sharking game. If you tell a man that he's beat, you are basically saying, "Fuck you, I don't respect you, and I don't believe you're going to do anything about it." Once that happens the code dictates that you "straighten" that. In other words, you put steel in him. If you don't, you become prey.

I didn't know what the true situation was with Zakil. I didn't know why he gave the money to Prince to pay me. Either way, I figured it was an opportunity to point out to him that Prince didn't have his best interests at heart—a real friend wouldn't take his money and gamble it away. Besides, I suspected that Prince only did this to take a jab at me. Since I doubted that Zakil knew the details about my history with Prince, I made my mind up to tell him everything and then waive the debt and give him a fresh start. I hoped it would be a lesson for him.

I walked over to his cell and tapped on the door. I could see from his face and body language that he was deeply distressed. "What's up?" I said, to break the ice. "Man, I told you I'm gonna pay you," he answered. "Don't keep sweating me about that shit." Suddenly, I felt defensive. "Sweating you? Man, ain't nobody sweating you. I just came over here to see what was up." In retrospect, I think we both misunderstood each other because everything went downhill after that. He snapped. I can't remember everything he said but it went something like this: "I already told you what the fuck was up. But you wanna keep sweating me, then fuck it, you beat nigga! I ain't paying you shit. Now get the fuck away from my door!"

I may have said something after that, I can't remember, but without a doubt, I was about to explode. This could no longer be resolved. He'd uttered the forbidden words. He told me I was beat. Which meant I had to put steel in him. There were no other options. It was in that moment that I made the decision in my heart to murder Zakil.

He was on lock-up in his cell, so I physically couldn't get to him. I would have to wait until he got off lock-up or they opened his door for a shower. Being that it was a Friday, I knew he wouldn't get off lock-up until Monday at the earliest. I was too anxious to wait, so I decided that as soon as he came out for a shower, I was gonna stab him.

I waited all day Saturday, but he told the CO he didn't want a shower that day. I had at least three people separately warn me that Zakil had asked them for a shank because he had beef with me. This only infuriated me more. There was only one way this was gonna end: somebody was getting stabbed. He wasn't gonna back down, he wasn't gonna apologize. He knew what the code dictated. It was like he was telling me, "Fuck you, I don't believe you are gonna do anything, and if you try, I think I can win."

Sunday afternoon, August 18, I made plans to go to the yard around 1 p.m. to set down the Georgia Skin game. Before I went outside, I told this white guy named Joey to let me know if Zakil came out of his cell for a shower. I went outside with my shank hidden in my construction work gloves and tucked in my right back pocket, like always. I set up the game and the players flocked. There were six or seven players. The guy with the glass eye was one of them. It was hot, and the yard was packed. After about an hour and a half, a guy named Intel came up and told me he needed to talk. He said to meet him over at the pull-up bar—it was very important.

I walked over about five minutes later, and he was with three other guys: Prince, a guy named Jay, and a guy named Mack. Intel told me that some-one named Zakil was asking around for a shank because he had beef with

Rome—me. Something about how he owed Rome money and wasn't gonna pay him and needed a shank. Then he told me that one of these guys (Prince, Jay, or Mack) had sold Zakil a shank only moments ago and he called me over because me and him was cool and he wanted me to know what was going on. Mack explained that he didn't want no problems, that he didn't even know who I was until right now. I knew Prince was orchestrating all this. I just nodded and said, "Okay," and went back to the Georgia Skin game. If there was any doubt in my mind before that moment, this removed it. *I have to put steel in him now*, I thought. On sight.

Only minutes later Joey walked up to me at the card table and said, "That boy's in the shower." I nodded, finished the hand, and called a guy named Redman to run the game. I had lost the entire sixty dollars I had, but that was the furthest thing from my mind.

I entered the building and made my way to A-Block. There were at least a dozen people in the hall waiting in the canteen line. I signaled for the CO to open the door. I could see through the window that someone was in the shower—I knew it was Zakil. Once I stepped into the shower area, I reached in my back pocket, pulled out the glove, removed the shank, and moved toward Zakil. He saw me. As I advanced, he said, "I'm gonna pay you your money, man!" But in my mind, it was too late. I stabbed him, again and again, until he collapsed, and then I started kicking him in his head.

The commotion attracted the guards, and from the corner of my eye, I saw a CO stick his arm in and start spraying mace. I turned away and searched the floor for my shank, which had slipped from my hand. I found it, picked it up and walked back to where Zakil laid on the floor and plunged the knife into his torso two or three times, but he showed no response. I went back over to the door and slid the shank toward the guards so they could see I was giving myself up. I walked out and they put me in handcuffs. I later learned that another shank was found on the shower floor. It undoubtedly belonged to Zakil, but he never got a chance to use it.

At the time, I honestly felt that I did what I was supposed to do—what was expected of me. I had no conscience. Not even a twinge of guilt. I even claimed that I had acted in self-defense. That was like a spit in the eye to Zakil and his family. It wasn't until I went to trial that anything like remorse entered my heart. I saw his mother and his grandmother. They testified about the son and grandson they knew, and for the first time I began to see Zakil as Dwayne Caldwell. I began to see him much like my mother saw me: as a human being, someone who was loved and who loved back. He wasn't just somebody that beat me out of a loan. When I realized that, and how easily the situation could be reversed, it finally hit me what I had done. His mother was grieving for him. My mother would be feeling the exact same way.

There is no justification for what I did. I am truly ashamed of this. I was a murderer and a liar, and the jury justifiably sentenced me to die. While I can never undo the harm I have caused, I am truly sorry, and I accept whatever punishment Allah has decreed for me. For now, I'm living with the consequences of my actions, having spent more than thirty years in prison, a quarter-century on Death Row.

Mercy on My Soul

It took the jury over four hours, feelin' so helpless with no
   power
In my throat I could taste it was sour
I watched the jury for some clue but their faces were dour
Sitting with his hands entwined on the table
The judge spoke, his voice was authoritative and stable
"Has the jury reached a verdict?" I gazed at the panel
An older white man in his sixties, my fate was a gamble
Not the type that lived by the code of the streets
The golfer type that brushes shoulders with social elites
"Yes, your honor," the foreman responded
I cast a glance at my attorney, his face was despondent
The bailiff passed the verdict along to the clerk
As she passed it to the judge, I witnessed a smirk

He peered over his glasses with a pompous air
And as he glared in condescension I mumbled a prayer

Lord have mercy on me, Lord have mercy on me
Mercy on my soul, I don't wanna live too old
But I don't wanna die this cold
Have mercy on me

I cast my view out at the spectators'
Faces to reflect on and assess later
My mother and my sister were seated behind me
The only people in the world that were clearly beside me
My mother looked so dignified in her best sweater
With her blue eyes she smiled, concealing her pain to make me
    feel better
She held my sister's hand and she squeezed it so tightly
My baby sister was my heart and she looked just like me
But on the other side where my vision averted
Was the grieving family of the man that I murdered
His mother had a look like a dagger of hate
Handkerchief clinched in her fist sadly dabbing her face
I swear it made my stomach churn and feel nauseous
My soul ached and my heart ripped from the guilt stabbin' my
    conscience
Snot leaked from my nostrils, I slumped down in my posture
And deep inside I prayed again from the very depths of my
    conscious

Lord have mercy on me, Lord have mercy on me
Mercy on my soul, I don't wanna live too old
But I don't wanna die this cold
Have mercy on me

As the judge perched on his throne
My heart thumped in my chest and I never felt so alone
The judge told me to stand up, I could hear disgrace in his tone
My knees were weak and I trembled as I stood to face the
    unknown
He said, "The jury having found the defendant himself

guilty of murder, and recommend the defendant be kept
at Central Prison," and before he could finish his breath
his gavel thundered as he issued a sentence of death!
My soul swirled as my world began to implode
My mother mouthed "I love you" as her tears began to explode
She reached for me as a deputy pulled me away from her hold
Last thing I heard was the judge's words, "May God have mercy
    on your soul"

PART II

Welcome to Death Row

Welcome to Death Row this is your resident Deadman talking
Your host to guide you close inside this world that I am
    walking
Your tour guide to peep into the minds of those who live it
A sentence reserved for less than one percent of the murders
    committed
The odds which are similar to one being struck by lightning
Yet being stuck by poison is a prospect just as frightening

However, walk with me as I describe the insides
The state-of-the-art facilities designed solely to end lives
In fact, I'd have to say this place looks quite medicinal
Sanitized to hide its use for executing criminals
As you enter, two remote controlled doors close right behind
    you

With an echoed metal clap perhaps just to remind you
That you can't leave so breathe and just leave that world
     behind you
As we walk through the valley of death I'm here to guide you
'Cause this is Death Row. Welcome to Death Row.

Okay, that first door, the one that's on your right, that would
     be the chaplain
The first office you come to and ironically the last when
Your date comes and perhaps you may need some spiritual
     guidance
To usher you into the next life, these accommodations are
     provided
The next door, the one that's to your left, that's a command
     post
For the sergeants and lieutenant and the first place every man
     goes
When he comes in to learn in which cell he'll be located
And also where the sergeant has you briefly orientated
Rules are rules! Now come with me as we walk through the
     hallway
See the cameras in the ceiling? They record and monitor all
     day
And to our left here is an alcove for therapeutic and medical
     health
To help you cope with the loss of your hope for the next twenty
     years as you
Wait for your death
We have pills for that, don't worry you'll be fine
The exit door in the alcove is the door that will take you
     outside
To the rec yard for exercise for sport and jump and play
In an enclosed space with a stone wall for one full hour a day
And on the stone wall are towers, see the guards patrolling
     with guns
To ensure no one attempts to climb the wall or tries to run
That's a no-no, these guards are trained to shoot and aim to kill
So if anyone attempts to flee you best believe they will
'Cause this is Death Row. Welcome to Death Row.

Death Row dayroom, Central Prison.
Photo by Justin Cook.

Welcome to Death Row, now follow me as we exit the yard
Now make a right after the alcove so I can take you to what's
    called a pod
At first there is a control booth reinforced with shatterproof
    glass
Equipped with multiple monitors and two guards performing
    their task
Of operating the control panel which remotely open the doors
And there is another directly above it to operate on identical
    floors
Each control booth sits on an island of four pods, together
    there's eight
And this is where the condemned are housed till executed by
    the State
Each pod has twenty-four cells with a toilet, a sink, and a bed
Well, actually a steel plank and a pallet for each of the dead
Don't worry you'll have your board games and puzzles to
    distract your mind

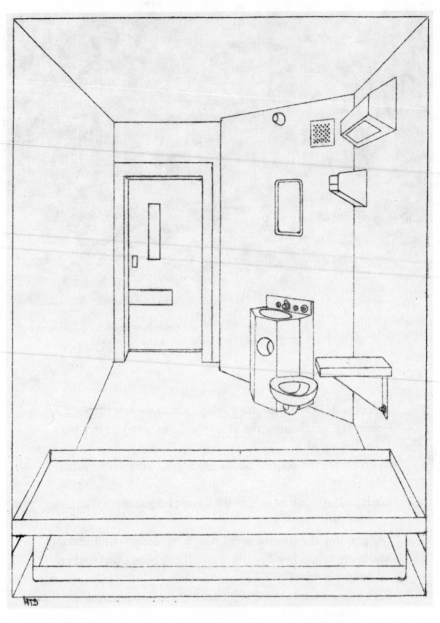

Death Row cell, Central Prison.
Drawing by Cerron T. Hooks.

Death chamber viewing room, Central Prison.
Photo by Justin Cook.

And even a snack from the canteen to help as you bide your
    time
Believe me we'll treat you humanely you'll hardly suffer an ill
And before your execution you can choose your own last meal
And when the moment comes you'll hardly feel a pain
During your ten-minute death, injecting poison in your veins
'Cause this is Death Row. Welcome to Death Row.

Death Row Is No Life of Luxury

N 2012, I WROTE to the *Gaston Gazette* in response to letter written by another Death Row inmate, Danny Hembree. Hembree had recently been sentenced to die and wrote that he was "a gentleman of leisure," living the good life on Death Row. He ended his letter by writing, "I laugh at you self-righteous clowns, and I spit in the face of your so-called justice system. Kill me if you can, suckers! Ha! Ha! Ha!" I wanted to explain what life was really like on Death Row, so I wrote this letter, which was published under the title, "Death Row Is No Life of Luxury":

I would like to respond to the recent media coverage concerning the conditions of life on Death Row. Despite what has been suggested by Danny Hembree, who does not speak for nor represent the views and opinions of those of us on Death Row, this is no life of leisure. In fact, Mr. Hembree had been on Death Row only two months when he wrote his letter claiming that he was a "gentleman of leisure watching color TV in the AC." This is certainly not what life is like on Death Row.

The true reality of life on Death Row is that every day is a life of fear, regret, and humiliation as a Death Row prisoner, my every day is consumed with the stress of waiting to die. Every moment is a countdown awaiting a court decision. I'm on edge every time my name is called for a legal visit. I'm afraid of receiving that letter stating that another round of my appeals has been denied, bringing me closer to that final moment. This is no life of leisure.

I am a man who is not trusted. Not believed. I am always a suspect. When an infraction is committed, I have no presumption of innocence. I've lost friends and associates in society who now view me disgracefully, as a convicted murderer unworthy to live. I'm housed in a special management unit solely for the condemned.

I don't enjoy the privileges that most general population prisoners are allowed. While most are allowed contact visits, all of my visits are behind glass with absolutely no contact. While other prisoners are allowed frequent telephone privileges, I am permitted one 10-minute phone call a year to my relatives. There are no rehabilitative programs to occupy my time like other prisoners are allowed. No AA, educational classes, no jobs.

Instead, I live in a cell the size of a bathroom. My window provides the view only of the prison. I'm allowed no more than two cubic feet of personal property, and my every day is spent literally waiting to die. Since I have been here, I've witnessed many men escorted to the death chamber over the years, never to return. Mr. Hembree has no idea what it's like to witness this walk of no return, and the hushed terror stamped into the eyes of every face that sees it.

This is no life of luxury, and I am no gentleman of leisure. I live every day with the fear of standing before my God and accounting for my deeds. My days and nights are filled with regret. Regret for the hurt I have caused and the lives I have ruined, including my own. Any comforts that I have been afforded, whether it's the privilege of being allowed to watch television or being protected from the elements of the cold or heat, are mercies that I am grateful for. Not something that I am audacious enough to say I deserve, but a mercy for someone waiting to die.

Years in Segregation

SPENT SEVEN AND A HALF YEARS in segregation, from August 1996 to February 2004. It was the darkest and most depressing time of my life. I reached a point where I lost all hope, and I'm ashamed to say it, but I wanted to die. It was the only solution I could come up with to end the misery and pain. I thank Allah for saving me just in time, because I don't think I would've made it another six months.

I rarely talk about this time because people just can't imagine the world I once lived in. I try to avoid even thinking about it because I don't like reliving those feelings. Especially the fear. The deepest scars on my mind and heart came from the countless times I witnessed guards beating inmates. Hearing a man's cries and the sounds of batons striking flesh. Hearing bodies hitting steel and concrete. Seeing inmates covered in blood. Eyes swollen shut. Teeth knocked out. Bodies covered in bruises. Standing alone in my cell feeling helpless. Afraid that if I spoke too loud and condemned what they were doing that I might be next. And the feeling, that crushing feeling deep down in your soul, that comes from turning a blind eye or a deaf ear because you don't want it to be you. Man, that's stuff I'm ashamed to talk about to this day.

I often thought about what it would be like to be executed. I shared my fears with my mother in a letter in January 1998, not long after I received my death sentence. At the time my execution date was set for February 8, 1998, although my legal appeal soon changed that. It was in that heightened state of fear and uncertainty that I wrote the letter:

> I am beginning to feel sure that I may die in the gas chamber. That would be an awful and painful death. I've read that it causes you to foam at the mouth while you're gasping for air, being strangled for life. Very awful. I never imagined dying like that, helpless. While people are watching me struggle with death until it conquers me and takes away my soul, this is awful. That is so demeaning to a man to have spectators watching while he is foaming at the mouth, choking from death. Also, there is the lethal injection, which is said to be a lot less painful, but it is the equivalent of surrender. From what I understand, you must request this penalty. What person would actually ask for the murderer to kill him a certain way and sign a form approving it? I think about all of this often. I don't know if I will escape it, and I don't really know if I care. I'm tired of all the pain, all the hurt, all the days, minutes, years of my life sitting in a cage. I'm tired of everything.

This was just a few weeks before Ricky Lee Sanderson was executed in the gas chamber. I was twenty-four years old and still had six years in the hole ahead of me.

My years in segregation broke me. It festered so much hate in my heart. I lived, breathed, and dreamed nothing but hate. My mind thought only of violence and murder. I hated the guards. I hated the inmates. I hated the system. I hated society. I hated everything. Everything around me and inside me was darkness. It was so dark I couldn't tell up from down.

I wrote rhymes during that time, but I hardly ever let anyone hear them because they're so cold, violent, and hate-filled. I keep some of them so I never forget. And others I have memorized, and they are a part of me like my arm. It was therapeutic to get the anger and the hate out, to put it on paper and then recite it. It helped me get the feelings out of my system a little at a time, every rhyme and every recitation, until my heart was empty and I could cope a little better.

Islam and Black Nationalism

OR THE FIRST SIX MONTHS after I was sentenced to death, I was in a state of shock. I could hardly get out of bed. All I did was eat and sleep and lay there reliving my memories. I was back in Raleigh, this time in Central Prison. I could look out my cell window and see cars driving up and down Western Blvd. and remember the countless times I passed this place. I grew up just two miles away in Kentwood. Now here I was sitting on Death Row.

I told myself that I had to rise up from this gloomy depression, but I was sapped. I needed something to draw energy from, something to motivate me. I needed focus and something to believe in. While at Blanch in 1994 I had become a Five Percenter, and by late 1995 I had gradually aligned myself with the teachings of the Nation of Islam under Louis Farrakhan. But in 1996 when I arrived at Caledonia, I put that knowledge on the back burner. I needed to adapt to my environment, so I reverted to that gangster life. Now that I was back in solitary confinement and this time with a death sentence, I began to reindoctrinate myself with the teachings of Elijah Muhammad.

Before coming to prison in 1993 I had never heard of Elijah Muhammad, Louis Farrakhan, or the Nation of Islam, and I knew nothing about the Five Percenters. It was while I was at Polk that I first became acquainted with them. My man Apple introduced me to his close friend from New York, Little Mas. I had heard about Little Mas on the street. He was infamous. A few months prior I had met his older brother, Big Mas, in the county jail and we became friends. The brothers had come down from New York to set up shop in Raleigh. Rumor had it that Big Mas moved dozens of kilos of crack by sending his workers packages on consignment and then having Little Mas go on the blocks and rob all the workers. When the workers told Big Mas they had been robbed, he gave them more crack to sell to work their debt off, in effect forcing them to work for him for free. As a result, the brothers were feared in the street. Little Mas was so well-known for robberies and shootings that anytime someone got robbed or shot on the streets, he was credited—whether he was the culprit or not. One of the jokes at the time was that if someone announced on the block, "Here comes Little Mas," people would run faster than if someone yelled "Police!"

While Big Mas was large and muscular, Little Mas was physically unintimidating. I used to hear people talking about fucking him up when they saw him, especially the drug dealers he had allegedly robbed. People claimed that he couldn't fight without his gun, but I used to see him on the yard at Polk alone or with one or two others, and nobody was stepping to him. When Apple introduced me to him, we formed an immediate bond based on mutual respect for how the other carried himself.

It was from Little Mas that I first learned some of the teachings of the Five Percenters. At the time I identified myself as a Hebrew Israelite, an identity that I had adopted in 1991 while I was doing time at Triangle Correctional Center in Raleigh. Mas was considered one of the most knowledgeable Five Percenters at Polk, and he was responsible for introducing many to the Five Percent Nation. He also had a healthy respect for my knowledge of the Bible and would often ask me where to find certain verses. Sometimes while we were talking a Five Percenter would come up and engage Mas in conversation, and I would listen. (They would greet each other by saying, "Peace God," which I thought was weird at the time.) The things that stood out in my mind the most were the names I had never heard before: Elijah Muhammad, Louis Farrakhan, Master Fard Muhammad, Clarence 13X, and

Malcolm X. I didn't like being ignorant. I couldn't understand why they thought of themselves as God, but I wanted to know why. But before I could delve too far into the knowledge of what they were teaching, I was shipped out to Blanch because I assaulted a guard.

While at Blanch in late 1994, it seemed like more than half the people on max were Five Percenters. I would lay back in my cell and listen to them build. It was fascinating. The way they spoke was intellectual and coded, and I wanted to unravel the mysteries of their mesmerizing wisdom. What intrigued me the most were their discussions about God and the devil. They said that the true God was the Asiatic Black man, the Supreme Being. They said the word "Being" means to exist and that man was the highest form of existence in the universe. Being that the Black man was the original man and that all other beings came from him, he was the Supreme Being, Father of Civilization, and God of the universe. They said that the white man was grafted from the original Black man through a process of separating the weaker of two germs in the Black man's sperm, and by grafting the weaker germ until it was no longer original. For this reason, the white race was called "mankind" by the Five Percenters because they were a *kind of man* grafted from the original. This process, they said, took six hundred years and was developed by a Black scientist named Yacub. According to the Five Percenters, Yacub was intent on making a new race of people who would be naturally weak and wicked. Through lies and deceit, he would teach them how to overpower and rule the original people of the planet Earth for six thousand years. After that time, the Black man would regain knowledge of himself and destroy the devil. According to the Five Percenters that time was now. I was deeply curious about this "secret knowledge," just as I had previously learned as a Hebrew Israelite that the truth was hidden in books.

Because my mother was white, I wasn't sure if I would be accepted by the Five Percenters. I talked to my friend Supreme, a Five Percenter, and asked him how the Fives classified a person whose mother was white. I was surprised when he told me that Master Fard Muhammad's mother was white. It was explained to me like this. According to the Five Percenters there are twenty-three wise Black scientists that are born every twenty-five thousand years, and together they write the history of everything that is to occur during that twenty-five-thousand-year period. That writing is kept in what is called the Mother Book and revealed only when a portion is about to be fulfilled. According to them, this is the origin of the Qur'an and the Bible. Supreme explained to me that Master Fard Muhammad's father was one of those twenty-three scientists and that once he learned that his people had been brought to America and enslaved, he wanted to come and teach us but couldn't because he was too dark. So he got a wife from the Caucasus Mountains in order to have a son who would look white, and he (the son) would deliver the knowledge of our true self. This man, Fard Muhammad, is reported to have begun teaching in Detroit in 1930, posing as a silk merchant and going door to door in the poorest part of the city. His star pupil was Elijah Poole. Poole would eventually become known as Elijah Muhammad, and after Fard Muhammad's disappearance in 1934, Elijah Muhammad would go on to lead the Nation of Islam for the next forty years. He became the teacher and spiritual leader for Malcom X, Louis Farrakhan, Muhammad Ali, and Clarence 13X—founder of the Five Percenters.

I was curious that Fard Muhammad was so revered by the Nation of Islam and yet had a white mother and a Black father, just like me. Whenever I listened to the Five Percenters talk, they referred to all white people as devils, but when they spoke about Fard Muhammad's mother, they never referred to her as a devil. She was considered righteous. All this intrigued me.

As much as I wanted to learn more about the Five Percenters, I couldn't get access to their knowledge unless I joined. The main problem was that I still believed in God and couldn't wrap my mind around the idea that I was God. However, there was a verse that I had read in the Bible, Psalms 82:6, that says, "I have said, Ye are gods; and all of you are children of the most High." Perhaps there was some deeper understanding that I had yet to gain, so I prayed to God for guidance. I told him that I did not intend to go astray, but I wanted to discover the truth. After I prayed on it and found the contentment in my heart, I told Supreme I wanted to join the Five Percenters. "That's a blessing," he said, and he became my enlightener.

I was thirsty and wanted every sip of knowledge I could get. The Five Percenters had a methodology for teaching based on memorization. You had to thoroughly memorize your lesson before you could advance to the next degree. The lessons were called One Twenty, which was known as the Book of Life. It is a series of 120 questions and answers as well as statements and alleged facts. The first official lesson that a Five Percenter receives is called Supreme Mathematics. According to the Five Percenters, Islam is mathematics, and mathematics is the science of everything in life. By mastering mathematics, one obtains the key to being. The Five Percenters would say that "Islam" is an acronym for "I Self Lord And Master."

The Supreme Mathematics is a system of numbers and their symbolic representations that orients the mind to connect everything in the universe to Five Percenter theology. Each number, 0 through 9, refers to a different principle: 1 is Knowledge, 2 is Wisdom, 3 is Understanding, 4 is Culture/Freedom, 5 is Power/Refinement, 6 is Equality, 7 is God, 8 is Build/Destroy, 9 is Born, and 0 is Cipher. An interesting feature of the Supreme Mathematics is that any multidigit number can be reduced to a single digit and represented by a that digit's corresponding principle. Take the number 111. To "born" this number, or reduce it to a single digit, you add the individual numbers, which makes 3 (1+1+1). So 111 is "born" to 3, and 3 is understanding. The number 97 becomes 16 (9+7), and then 16 becomes 7 (1+6), and 7 represents God. I was fascinated by this principle and applied it to everything I encountered. If I saw a number, no matter what or where, I would "born" it and manifest the science behind it.

As I progressed in my memorization of the lessons, I was eager to learn more about how the white race was grafted from the Black man. One day I was listening to a Five Percenter named Shaka as he talked about the grafting process. I asked him if he knew of a book that I could order that broke down how the white man was made. He told me that Elijah Muhammad described the whole process in his 1965 book, *Message to the Blackman in America*. I asked Shaka how come Elijah Muhammad knew so much about it, and he looked at me from behind his door like I was crazy. He said, "Elijah Muhammad wrote the lessons."

I was stunned. I ordered *Message to the Blackman* that night. When it arrived, I read it cover to cover, and my knowledge increased a hundredfold. I was awed. Elijah Muhammad not only talked about theology and the making of the white race, he talked about economic development, Black independence and self-reliance, and the ownership of land. He made a strong argument for reparations and separation of the races. He said that since Black people had built this country through slave labor, they were entitled to a portion of the wealth that had accrued. He said that emancipation from slavery meant nothing when the Black man was still dependent on his former master for sustenance. The Black man was not free when he relied on his former master for a job. He had no land of his own to cultivate. The food that he ate was grown on the white man's land. If the white man refused to employ him or refused to sell to him, what good was his freedom? Elijah Muhammad said that the government of the United States should set aside a few states for its former slaves and their descendants, or resettle them somewhere else in the world and provide aid for them for twenty years until they were able to do for themselves. He said that he was a Messenger from Allah, and that Allah had raised him up from ignorance and had commissioned him to preach and resurrect the dead Negro in America.

I had never heard anything as strong and powerful as what Elijah Muhammad said. He seemed to be the wisest man in the universe. Plus, he claimed to be the Messenger of God and was disclosing alleged realities that had been hidden from the world for thousands of years. I was hypnotized.

His teachings had all the markings of a cult, only I didn't know what a cult was. But I decided that it made more sense to follow Elijah Muhammad since he was the author of the very lessons that the Five Percenters followed. Besides, the things Elijah Muhammad taught were more enlightening to me than anything I heard from the Five Percenters. So in January 1996, I left the Five Percenters and became an unregistered member of the Nation of Islam, which is what I would adhere to for at least the next seven years. It wasn't until I was on the brink of the pit of fire, contemplating death, that Allah opened my heart to the true light of Islam as taught by his final Prophet Muhammad ibn Abdullah to whom the Holy Qur'an was revealed in Mecca, Arabia over 1,400 years ago.

Allahu Akbar!

URING MY YEARS IN SEGREGATION, I could see no end to my pain and felt that my very existence held no purpose. This idea was rooted in the teachings of Elijah Muhammad, who told his followers that there was no life after death. Heaven and hell were conditions of life, and when you were dead, it was over. But if this were true, I wondered, what difference did it make if I lived a righteous life or not? Why continue living at all? As my mind yielded to hopelessness, I started fantasizing about death. Plotting it even. I imagined going out in a blaze of glory like George Jackson—the author of the book *Soledad Brother*, who was killed while trying to escape from San Quentin in 1971. If I could do that, I thought, my legacy would be immortalized.

The more I thought about death, however, the more I began to wonder if there was anything on the other side. The universe seemed to be too purposeful for my life to have no meaning. I had been taught to believe in the Qur'an, and I'd read it at least seven times by then. It was replete with verses that described the resurrection, the Day of Judgment, and life after death in paradise or hell. However, Elijah Muhammad taught that these verses referred to the spiritual and mental resurrection of Black people. I had always glossed over those explanations in the past, but now they simply didn't make sense.

The Qur'an says: "He [Allah] has created him [man], then molded him in due proportions. Then does He make his path smooth for him. Then He causes him to die and puts him in a grave. Then when it is His will, He will raise him up (again)" (80:17–22). The Qur'an also says: "It is Allah who gives life, then gives death, then He will gather you together for the Day of Judgment about which there is no doubt, but most men do not understand" (45:24–26). These and other verses gripped my soul and refuted the message that Elijah Muhammad preached. Suddenly his teachings came tumbling down like a house of straws, leaving me lost and confused. It was in that state of mind that I was unexpectedly released from Unit One in 2004, after more than seven years in segregation.

Several life-impacting events happened within the first months of my departure from both Unit One and the Nation of Islam, beginning with the death of a friend who was killed right after I left solitary. He grabbed an officer's gun during a court appearance and shot a correctional officer before being gunned down by police. I felt morally responsible because I'd been preaching Elijah Muhammad's idea that there was no life after death to him before I was released from lock-up. His death seemed pointless. No one viewed him as a George Jackson. Hardly anyone remembers him at all.

A few months later, the state of North Carolina began executing people at a rapid rate. There had been twenty-three executions within a six-year span while I was on Unit One, but between October 2004 and August 2006, twelve people were executed, starting with three in just five weeks. Death loomed all around me. I began popping pills, drinking wine, and playing poker to escape the stress.

By the grace of Allah, a moratorium on executions went into effect in August 2006, and the following year I met a Muslim woman through a pen pal site and fell in love. By 2010 our relationship was over, but it was through her that I began to rekindle my connection with Islam. While I had considered myself a Muslim since 1996, I had never practiced true Islam, and I was still in a spiritual no-man's-land after leaving the Nation of Islam in 2003.

I needed Allah. I needed His guidance, His forgiveness, and His mercy, and I needed to surrender myself completely to Him. But I couldn't do it alone. So I moved to another pod and connected with a brother named Ali. I asked him if he performed the five daily prayers known as salat. He told me he did, and I asked him if he would come and get me for each prayer and pray with me. He agreed, and, Alhamdulillah, here I am many years later with my faith as strong as ever.

In 2012 I was elected imam for Death Row's Muslims, and the first and most important thing that I did was to establish congregational salat on each pod. Prior to that, the Muslims on Death Row who did pray performed their prayers alone in their cells. But I understood the power of congregational prayer and urged the Muslims to pray salat together in their pods. To this day it is my greatest achievement. Alhamdulillah!

I believe in the Oneness of God, His angels, His books, His prophets, life after death, and the Divine Decree. I pray and I fast for Ramadan, and I adhere to the recipe for success in this life and the Hereafter: belief in Allah and doing good deeds. Islam is the greatest thing that has ever happened to me, and I am so grateful for Allah's guidance and mercy. Allah is the greatest! Allahu Akbar!

Living among the Innocent

WHEN I GOT TO Death Row, I expected that everybody would be just like me. People with multiple murders. People who had killed in cold blood. The absolute worst of the worst. I was prepared for that. But what I was not prepared for—what never even crossed my mind as a possibility—was that there would be innocent people on Death Row.

There have been six people in North Carolina who have been found innocent and who went home after spending years on Death Row since I've been here: Alfred Rivera, Alan Gell, Jonathan Hoffman, Levon Jones, Edward Chapman, and Henry McCollum. I didn't really know the first five because I was on lock-up for seven and a half years and didn't get out until 2004. Hoffman, Gell, and Rivera were already gone by then, so I never met them. Jones and Chapman I saw, but we didn't talk much. I didn't know anything about their cases, so when they left it didn't impact me much. But Henry McCollum changed my perspective.

I knew Henry. We weren't close friends, but we lived on the same unit for at least ten years. He was quiet, slow, and very timid. I heard about his case—he had been charged with raping and killing an eleven-year-old girl. He claimed he was innocent, but I didn't believe him. I thought he was a sick pervert in denial and I didn't have any sympathy for him. But to my utter disbelief, around the end of August 2014 people started saying that Henry was getting ready to go home. His case was being brought before the Innocence Inquiry Commission, and they were saying that he really was innocent.

I started to take an interest in his case and talked to him. I found out that his brother, Leon Brown, who was also convicted and originally sentenced to death along with Henry in 1984 but had then gotten resentenced to life, had filed a complaint with the Innocence Inquiry Commission. Actually, another inmate had filed on his brother's behalf, because his brother could hardly read or write. The commission investigated the claim and, for the first time, sent DNA evidence to be tested. Lo and behold, the DNA implicated another man who had been arrested for a similar murder and rape less than a month after Henry and his brother had been arrested. That man, Artis Roscoe, had been sentenced to death and had spent years on Death Row with Henry and his brother. He had even befriended them, knowing all along that they were innocent.

It was only because of Leon Brown's petition that both brothers were eventually exonerated. The commission only investigates claims of innocence from people who have exhausted all their appeal options in court. A person on Death Row can never file a petition to the commission, because as long as a person is on Death Row, they are still under appeal. When a Death Row prisoner has no more appeal options, he is executed. So Henry could've never filed a petition to the commission, and therefore the only way he was able to have his case heard was because the commission was hearing his brother's case and they were codefendants.

When I found out that Henry was innocent, I felt guilty because I had condemned him along with everyone else. It broke my heart as I tried to put myself in his shoes and imagine what it had been like for him for over thirty years—accused of a horrible crime that he didn't commit. And his brother was only fifteen years old. With a crime like that, he was attacked and raped repeatedly over the years. I sat in my cell, and I cried for those brothers and what they went through. There's no compensation for that. Nothing that can ever restore what was taken from them.

Henry McCollum was the sixth person who went home from Death Row after being wrongfully convicted since I've been in Central Prison. I realized that the system was flawed. No, that's an understatement. It was broken. I already knew about Elrico Fowler's case. He had told me about his innocence around 2013. This blew my mind because I met him in 1998 and we had become good friends. Yet for fifteen years he had never told me he was innocent. I didn't understand it at first. Why didn't he tell me? Because he thought I already knew. I went back through my mind and recounted the hundreds of conversations we'd had and with the knowledge that he was innocent in mind, they all started to take on a different meaning. He had been telling me this the whole time, but I wasn't listening. I said to myself, "Alim, you've got to start paying attention to what people are really saying." Since then, I've met several people on Death Row that I believe really are innocent. I think about all the people that drive by this prison every day—right in the heart of Raleigh—who have no idea that innocent people are behind these walls. Innocent people sitting in cells on Death Row waiting to be executed. Innocent people feeling utterly helpless as the gigantic machine that is the justice system churns away with pitiless routine.

Once I woke up to the reality that there are innocent people living with me here on Death Row, I started to see things differently. I've learned that they can adapt to their environment and survive. They learn the rules, mimic some of the conduct of those around them. Even develop some of the attitude, the facial expressions, and tone. They can learn to look tough, act tough, blend in, and seem unfazed. But the fact is, you can't disguise yourself as a killer when you are surrounded by them. You'll get sniffed out like a virgin in a room full of pimps. And that's facts. My friend Sabur is innocent. The man ain't never killed nobody. One of the reasons I know is because when you do actually kill someone you lose an innocence that you can never regain. And just talking to Sabur sometimes reminds me of the innocence that I once had. It's a way of seeing the world that you never appreciate until it is lost. And once it's lost, it never comes back. When I talk to my mom I still can see and hear that innocence in her, and it's also in Sabur. They don't even know it's there. But I do.

I feel a moral responsibility to do something. How can I not? I'm supposed to be here. I know what I deserve. I'm guilty. But when I look around and I see people in here like Elrico and Sabur, it's like, *WAIT! Hold up! These men aren't supposed to be here.* I can't just act like nothing is happening. I ain't built like that. The least I can do is call out for help. The least I can do is scream at the top of my lungs, saying, "Hey! There are innocent people in here! They aren't supposed to be here. Somebody please help!" So that's what I'm trying to do with my music. I'm making some noise to bring attention to the fact that Elrico and Sabur are innocent. There are others too, but you've got to start somewhere.

There are four reasons for me to be making music. Either I'm doing it for fun, or I'm trying to make a difference in the world with my talent, or I'm doing it for money, or I'm doing it for fame. While there's nothing wrong with any of these motives, I'm primarily motivated by the first two. I love writing and reciting rhymes. It's my passion. It's fun, and it's an ability that Allah gave me. But at the end of my life, I don't want to feel like I've squandered what Allah has given me. I want my life's work to have real meaning. So that when I stand before my Lord and He asks me what I did with what He gave me I can say I used it to help people, and I pray that He will be pleased. And what greater meaning or nobler thing can you do than to save a person's life? Allah says in the Qur'an that to kill a person is like killing all of mankind, and to save one life is like saving all of mankind. Inshallah, if I can use my music to literally save a man's life on Death Row, then that's in the ultimate service of Allah. I may not accomplish this, but at least my Lord will know that I spent my time trying to make a difference and I pray that He will forgive me for the wrong I've done in my life.

Unbreakable

Ruff, ruff, ruff Raleigh made me tough probably
Took me and shaped me and mold me from a young Svengali
Taught me to thug it properly
Introduced me to drugs and parties and then seduced me with
    them hugs from hotties
Tuckin' them guns in robberies, bustin' them slugs from
    shotties
Then they seen me on a TV with a couple bodies
Threw me in a jail cell with my hombres
No ice grill but if looks could kill my eyes would tell you don't
    try me
When that door closed up behind me and them walls start to
    remind me that I'm all alone and I ain't goin' home and I
    ain't never huggin' my Mommy

They buried me beneath concrete eyebrow deep you can't find
    me
And I sat there in that cold cell staring at the ceiling like Why
    Me?
Now here I am after twenty years and I say Alhamdulillah!
Standing on the Sirat al-Mustaqeem and it's all praise to Allah
Never dreamed I'd make it this far but now I'm raising the bar
Kickin' doors down on Death Row like waaaaah!
They can't break me down
They can't break me down

Okay now let's go, most of y'all probably didn't know
The city's namesake was on Death Row
Two chops from the ax blow completely severed his head
So who better fit to represent my city, Sir Walter's back from
    the dead
And I made a vow and I swear to God I'ma keep on speaking
    that truth
And shine a light on this dark plight and those executed like
    "poof"
My man Henry did thirty years 'fore the system ever found
    proof
Of his innocence and then set him free after robbing him of his
    youth
So I looked around and started thinking outward
How to use my voice and start speaking louder
For those innocent and still in the trench like Stacey Tyler and
    Elrico Fowler
Stacey Tyler, Elrico Fowler!
Say them names and repeat 'em louder
I pray to God they get relief before God judge in that Final
    Hour
What makes it worse is I done seen a lot of cases worst
But I ain't seen too many men who wanna make amends like
    Jason Hurst
Who'll it face first? So many's died
They done executed at least thirty-five
Since '97 when I first arrived and I thank God I'm still alive

But I cannot turn a blind eye and just act like that everything's
    pretty
When we got people on Death Row right here in the heart of
    the city
And that's real life, no make-believe and no Hollywood
If I could change the world then I probably would
But I done did something nobody could, and . . .
They can't break me down
They can't break me down

My First Recordings

THERE'S NOTHING EASY ABOUT rapping over the phone, especially on a prison phone on Death Row. I sometimes feel awkward or self-conscious—as Erykah Badu once said, "I'm an artist, and I'm sensitive about my shit." If I'm rhyming to an audience, even if it's just a few people, I can feed off the crowd energy. When you look in someone's eyes and see that they are feeling you, nodding their head, or making expressions of awe, then that's motivation to kill it. But when I'm on the phone, there's no crowd. Usually, my back is to the dayroom. People are at a distance. I'm not sure if they are listening. Sometimes I hear them talking casually. Sometimes they are playing cards, or working out, and sometimes there's silence. It's hard under those circumstances to feel like you're giving your best performance. Sometimes I get in my head wondering if anybody is even paying attention, or maybe they think I'm wack. If I'm not going to have a real audience, I would prefer to be alone in a booth to just let go and give it everything I've got. Rapping on the phone in the dayroom, I sometimes hold back. I don't spit it like it was supposed to be spit. I don't put enough emotion in it. Still, sometimes people will come up to me later and say they liked a song I was doing earlier, and they might repeat a line. That always makes me feel better and motivates me for the next session. One guy jokingly calls me Suge Knight, the infamous CEO of Death Row Records. He'll say, "I heard you over there this morning, Suge Knight. You representin' Death Row!"

The first song I recorded over the phone and posted on SoundCloud was "Round My Way." I wrote that song maybe a week or two before recording it. I didn't have the courage to record my best stuff first because if nobody liked it, I would've been crushed. So I put out "Round My Way," and people liked it! My brother Chris—Doc, as I call him—is my number one fan on the outside. According to SoundCloud, he's listened to "Round My Way" over seven hundred times!

"Round My Way" was just an a cappella, and the feedback I kept receiving was that I needed to put it to a beat. I reached out to people to see if they could help, but I kept getting the same response: my timing was off. I didn't understand. If my timing was off, why couldn't they adjust the music to my tempo? I concluded that they must be amateurs. I figured a real producer could make it work. I kept recording and released more a cappellas. After a few months I linked up with a Raleigh producer named DJ Dezerk. We talked a couple of times on the phone, and he too explained that my timing was a problem. He said that my tempo was constantly changing, and I needed to record my a cappellas to a timed beat. For the first time it started to sink in that these producers weren't incompetent. My timing really was a problem.

I tried to figure out a way to overcome this obstacle but kept drawing blanks. I thought I had found the solution when DJ Dezerk played a beat from his computer over the phone so I could rap over it. But we soon discovered two problems. The first was that there is a slight delay on the phone, perhaps due to the calls being recorded. This would throw my rhythm off, making it very difficult to rap to. But the real problem was the second one. As soon as I started rapping all I could hear was my own voice being played back to me a second later like a huge echo. It completely drowned out the beat.

We went back to the drawing board. He suggested that I rap to a metronome. He played one over the phone and explained what it was. But it sounded weird—just a bunch of beeps—and I couldn't lock in with it. I felt like we were making no progress. I was wasting time and money since each call cost me eleven cents per minute, and I was spending hours on the phone. But one day I was listening to the radio, and I just started rapping "Round My Way" on top of another song. I realized that I could block out whatever was being sung and just rap to that beat. Perhaps that would solve the timing issue. At least my rhyme would be to a fixed tempo. I called DJ Dezerk and told him my idea. He said it was worth a try. I turned on my radio and waited for the next song to begin. I had no way of knowing what song was gonna be played and at what tempo. And I only had the three minutes or so that the average song plays on the radio. I couldn't mess up. I can't even remember what song came on. But I went in. I blocked out everything and made it my song. DJ Dezerk said we had a tape. He said my vocals came out good and he was gonna get to work on it right away. I was excited. I just knew that within a few weeks I was gonna be hearing myself on the radio! All I needed was a good beat.

A couple of weeks went by, and we had something. DJ Dezerk sent a skeleton version of a beat and my rhymes to my brother via email. Doc loved it. He played it every day. My mom said he literally kept it on repeat. Dezerk told me that he had let a few people hear it and they were already saying it had all the potential to be a hood anthem for Raleigh. I was stoked and ready to record something else. I told all my friends that I was about to release a song. And finally, that day came. It was May 29, 2019. I had my niece email the song to several local DJs. My mom asked me if I had heard it yet. I told her no. She said, "Well, your brother liked the original version better." "What do you mean?" I asked. She said he liked the skeleton beat and rhyme better than the final cut, and she agreed. I wanted to know what was different and she said I just needed to hear it. It took me about a month before I managed to find someone to play it for me. I was immediately disappointed. No shade on DJ Dezerk, but it didn't sound like the song I envisioned. It didn't have the beat that I had in my mind, and the sound quality of the vocals was poor. I felt resigned. I thought I would never be able to accomplish my dreams. Not because of my lack of talent, but because of my lack of access to quality technology.

All about the Money

THE PRISON PHONE IS my connection to the world, the reason people on the other side of the wall can hear me rap. But that access doesn't come cheap. In North Carolina, Global Tel Link has the exclusive contract for prison telephone calls. When I came to prison in 1993, you could make a local call for a quarter using the pay phone and talk for an hour or more. Collect calls were more expensive, but no calls were monitored or recorded. This seems unbelievable now because surveillance is so embedded in the system. If prison officials wanted to record someone's call because they suspected criminal activity, they had to get a warrant for a wiretap.

Companies like Global Tel Link saw a massive potential for profit from prison calls, but how could they convince prison systems to give them an exclusive contract? By offering, in the name of security, a means to monitor and record all phone conversations. But how could Global Tel Link monitor and record the calls? Isn't that illegal? It's only illegal when the person doesn't know they're being recorded. But if you tell them, it's legal. And that's what they do—at the beginning of every call, the lady says, "This call will be monitored and recorded." In exchange for providing this service, Global Tel Link gets a near monopoly on prison phone calls. And because of that, I pay much more than anyone on the outside pays. Phone calls cost me and my family about $200 a month. It costs me $1.61 to make a fifteen-minute local call, and that's a lot less than in other states.

Global Tel Link isn't the only company making money off incarcerated people. There's also JPay, which handles money transfers at many prisons. Before JPay took over, we would receive money orders directly from friends and family, and the money would be quickly deposited into our accounts. Money orders now have to be mailed to JPay's office in Florida for processing. JPay's pitch was that the prison could then focus more on inspecting mail for contraband. In addition, JPay would offer an electronic option for sending money. It's supposed to be a measure of convenience, but it's not. Before JPay, there were never significant delays in processing money orders. A money order might take a few days to get to me by mail, and once it arrived the money would be in my account the next day. But it takes JPay a month. And it has a monopoly over all the money transfers to prisons in North Carolina and in many other states as well. My mom pays JPay around ten dollars in service fees every time she sends me money, which is once a month. Imagine how much money JPay makes every month, and to do what? To simply serve as the middleman for our families to deposit money into our accounts. JPay took that sweetheart of a deal and parlayed its way into providing other services as well, including access to music, movies, video visitation, and phone calls.

Now, in addition to phone calls and money transfers, Central Prison outsources its mail service. Beginning in late 2021, it was no longer possible for family and friends to send mail directly to the prison. Instead, they send letters to a company called Text Behind, which then scans the letters and sends copies to the recipients. According to the official memorandum I received, this was done because of the problem of contraband and drugs coming through the mail. The memo made it sound like this was done for our benefit: "We anticipate less drug use, risk of overdose, and violence. It will also reduce the risk of accidental contact with dangerous drugs." While it is a fact that people send drugs into prison though the mail, that's only one way— and not the main way—drugs enter prison. Moving to Text Behind just imposes greater restrictions on the incoming mail for the 99 percent of people who aren't being sent drugs, and it opens up an opportunity for another business to profit off of us.

Just like JPay, Text Behind slows everything down. The time it takes to process a letter sent through the regular mail ends up taking so long that people feel forced to pay for the electronic option just to maintain contact with their loved ones. The electronic option is faster, but it always costs more, and it's not always more convenient. Before Text Behind took over, my coauthor Mark Katz would send me printouts of chapter drafts of this book through the regular mail for me to read and mark up. It only took a couple of days for his letters to get to me. With Text Behind, he could still send me printouts, but he had to send them to Maryland first, and it could take weeks for the copies to get to me. And sometimes the copies left out pages or put them in the wrong order. So you would think it would be better just to send things electronically. Not necessarily. On the outside, Katz could send someone a 250-page book manuscript in a single email. But when he sends me the equivalent of three pages, he has to break it into several texts, and each text costs money. Photos can also be sent, but only one at a time, each for a separate fee. And each message and photo must be individually approved, which can take hours or even days.

All these "services," whether provided by Global Tel Link, JPay, Text Behind, or some other company, were supposedly instituted for the sake of security and convenience. But it's really all about money, and I'm at a state institution, not a for-profit prison. Incarcerated people and their families are an easily exploited market. Of course, I'll pay whatever it costs to talk to my mom or Jeannie, and my family and friends have no choice but to pay whatever it costs to communicate with me. The companies and the prisons know this, and they capitalize on it. We are a goldmine, and everybody is trying to cash in on us.

Total Loss of Privacy

ONE OF THE CONSEQUENCES of imprisonment is the total loss of privacy. You don't even have the freedom to record and safeguard your own thoughts. In the past I've had my writings confiscated and never returned. I lost three albums of song lyrics like that back in 2000. The captain of Internal Affairs came and seized all my personal property for absolutely no reason. I was in segregation then and hadn't had a write-up in over three years. Then one day they came to my cell door, told me to strip and put my hands out to be cuffed. Then they put me in a holding cell and packed up all my property. They even took my mattress. They left me in the holding cell, just a cage big enough to stand in, for about six hours as the captain combed through every inch of my property. After he was done, he sent my property back on a cart and took me to my cell. They had cut my mattress open, so they brought me another mattress.

When I checked my property, I noticed that all my writings were missing. Everything—including all my rhymes. I was told that the captain had confiscated them. Why, I asked? Nobody knew. I wrote a grievance and finally got a response a couple weeks later: my writings were confiscated because they were considered a threat to security and order. What made them a threat to security and order? A single line in the song, "Original Gangster"—"I'm the one that made Bloods start hating Crips." Did the captain read the rest of the song? Did he know what it was about? The entire song is about the government. I'm rapping in first person as Uncle Sam, saying that I (Uncle Sam) am the Original Gangster. So when I say, "I'm the one that made Bloods start hating Crips," I'm accusing the government of promoting gang violence in the Black community. This is clear if you read all the lyrics. But I might as well have been talking to the wall because they weren't listening. Fortunately, I had memorized the song before it was stolen from me.

I finally said okay, if you want to confiscate that song even though I'm talking about the government, then what about the rest of my writings? I wasn't talking about gangs in the rest of my stuff, why can't I have it back? No response. I never got any of my writings back. Lost three albums of lyrics, most of which I hadn't memorized, including a song I wrote called "Black Messiah," one of my all-time favorites. I wrote it from the perspective of a fetus waiting to be born so he can save his people. But the way I'm describing it, you'd think that the protagonist is in prison waiting to be released. I started the song saying something like this: "I've got nine months till my release date falls / and I can finally break free from these walls / I'm coming out headfirst." Then I describe everything I'm gonna do to change the world. However, by the end of the song instead of being released I get sentenced to death. I describe being placed on a gurney and doctor standing around me with a syringe. It's actually an abortion, but I depict it like a lethal injection. I loved that song and put a lot of work into writing it. I never tried to rewrite it because I don't feel I can re-create it as good as the original. So it's just a lost song.

Original Gangster

I'm the Original Gangster y'all wankstas ain't real y'all artificial
I drop bombs while you featherweights be packin' pistols
I be blastin' missiles with my initials on my enemies across seas
I'm known to cop keys of coca through Nicaragua
My MO is armed robber
And drug trafficker
I'll smuggle M16s to South Africa
And make it snow like it came from Alaska
I own platinum mines, you own one ring and one necklace
You young and reckless with a Lexus
A money clip and Rolexes
While I transport tons to Texas and ship crack to Los Angeles
A continental vandalist
I kill niggas with randomness
You ain't know that I was scandalous?

Dress up like an evangelist then I'll brandish a revolver
That's the way I robbed your father
I'm not really bothered 'cause you murdered a cat
'Cause y'all was both smokin' my weed and y'all was both
    sellin' my crack
And them was my slugs and my gat
And besides y'all was both Black
You ain't real mack I invented the game
You just a player that claims my name, slangs my cane
Smokes weed and gangbangs
But yo I'm sayin', you ain't a killer you just fuss a lot
Get high and wanna cuss a lot
Pumpin' rocks while I lock states
You on the block tryin' to cop a big 8
While I negotiate contracts with my associates
To get Tec-9s and .38s
From gunmakers, aircrafts and tankers landmines and nines,
    coke by the acres
Big Sammy style, all y'all is fakers
There's only one Original Gangster

You ain't a thug, you just a player
You slang my drugs 'cause you work for me the Original
    Gangster
And everybody knows you're fakin' 'cause there's only one OG
And it's true every slug you bust really comes from me

I've done armed robberies
Stole niggas properties
Tricked half a billion and built up monopolies
Stacked cream
Made hookers out of Black queens
Spit game that turnt kings to crack fiends
Taking trips
Across seas making chips
Killin' cats before guns started taking clips
I'm the one that make Bloods start hating Crips
Word to mother
Killing cats for color

Gangbangin' fool and kidnappin' brothers
Straight jackin'
Big ballin' straight mackin'
Now you on the avenue .38 packin'
Talkin' like a thug but just actin'
See, you ain't really no criminal
Not the Original—
Gangster
This Thug Life's in my nature
You fakin' jacks ain't ya?
Nigga you ain't major
You only in the game as a player
I own half the globe
You only rock ice in your earlobe
That I stole with a shipload of gold
That I jacked from your brother, turned around and sold
Back to y'all
While you were drunk drinkin' alcohol
Smokin' reefer and tryin' to learn how to ball
And flex muscle
You can't knock the hustle
I got you in the chokehold, nigga call me uncle
Big Sammy style, all y'all is fakers
There's only one Original Gangster!

You ain't a thug, you just a player
You slang my drugs 'cause you work for me the Original
    Gangster
And everybody knows you're fakin' 'cause there's only one OG
And it's true every slug you bust really comes from me

By now possibly
I know all y'all probably
Wanna know what's my claim, what's my aim
Seeing how I floss on y'all like a G when I spit my game
I'm thugged out, "Say my name"
I thought you knew, but here's a clue
I'm the only G with gang colors both red and blue

With the star-spangled banner bandanna sewn in my clothes
    standing in a gangster pose
I suppose the globe knows I'm the shadiest
The world knows my alias
As Uncle Sam, I'm the United States player
I'm the Original Gangster!
You ain't a thug, you just a player
You slang my drugs 'cause you work for me the Original
    Gangster
And everybody knows you're fakin' 'cause there's only one OG
And it's true every slug you bust really comes from me

A Gangster Trying to Be Muslim

I ONCE TOLD MY FRIEND MU'MIN—the white Muslim from West Virginia who encouraged me to record my music—that every day for me is a jihad, a struggle. That's because at the time I was a gangster trying very hard to be a Muslim. I was still filtering all my actions and conduct through the Code of the Streets and the Convict Code. Outwardly, I wasn't part of the street culture or the penitentiary hustle anymore, and I was completely in submission to Allah. But I still adhered to some of that thinking. I wasn't in that life anymore, but I still wanted the admiration of those who were. It was the only currency to be salvaged from that life. It was my pension, so to speak.

So I had a jihad going on inside me. I was living for Allah. I was in a position of leadership as an imam. But occasionally, situations would put my faith in conflict with the Convict Code. For instance, there might arise a question about Muslims and snitching. How were we supposed to deal with members among our own ranks who were known or suspected snitches? I took the disassociation approach. That is, if a Muslim snitched on someone, I would stop associating with him. Snitching is taboo in prison, but it isn't necessarily a sin that Allah is gonna punish a person for. How could I rightfully disassociate myself from a Muslim when he hadn't done anything to incur Allah's displeasure? As my faith and understanding of the religion began to grow, I knew that I couldn't continue to straddle both worlds. They weren't reconcilable.

The first real test came when two Muslims got into a conflict and one of them put his hands on the other, hitting him in the face. I'll call them A. (the original instigator) and B. (the retaliator). Even though we broke up the fight immediately, B. vowed that it wasn't over. Maybe two months later, he came up behind A. and hit him in the head with a sock full of soap. Knocked him out cold. Somebody told me what happened, so I ran to the scene. A. was laid out on the floor with blood everywhere. I helped him up and eventually the guards came and took him to the hospital. He was badly injured. He still suffers intense headaches and for a while his hearing and eyesight were affected. After about a week, the guards came and locked up the other brother, B., and rumor went around that A. had snitched. Everybody was cursing his name. People were vowing that they were done with him, including most of the Muslims, a few highly respected Muslims, too.

I held my tongue. Honestly, I felt compassion for this brother. It hurt my heart to see him laid out on the floor like that, unconscious, bleeding profusely. He had fallen face first and broken his teeth. He'd been hospitalized. His hearing and vision were impaired. There was fear that his brain might swell or bleed and that could've led to death. Yet everybody was condemning *him*. Where was the compassion, especially from the Muslims? The experience opened my eyes. I realized that some people, hell, most people, cared more about adherence to the code than about someone's life. And why did they care so much? They didn't want people to think for one second that they condoned snitching. So they cursed the injured brother while he was still in the hospital, even suggesting that he got what he deserved.

Nobody tried to help A. I'm not suggesting that he was innocent in the situation—he hit the other brother first. But Islam says that an eye for an eye limits justice, and of course, it's best to forgive. And A. wasn't hit back in equal retaliation. He had been knocked out. What if that had been me? Would nobody help me? Would some of my brothers in faith wash their hands of me just to save face? That was a revelation. It showed me who was who and what was what.

This is what I did. I waited for A. to get back from the hospital and then had a talk with him. Straight up I said that I didn't think what happened to him was just. But I also told him he was wrong for putting his hands on that other brother. If nothing else, this should be a wake-up call that he can't go around hitting people. One day somebody might kill him. Then I told him that he needed to give up the life of this world of drugs and gambling and get on his deen—fulfill his religious obligations as a Muslim. I told him that if he is striving for Allah's pleasure and doing what is right, then I didn't care if everybody turned their backs on him. He was my Muslim brother, and I would have his back. I was reminded of the story of Noah in the Qur'an. Noah was sent by Allah to preach to the people to live good and pure lives. Most of the people opposed him and despised those who would follow him. Noah responded, "I will not drive away (in contempt) those who believe, for verily they are to meet their Lord, and I see you are the ignorant ones."

A. chose Allah, and I had his back. One time we were in the hallway and several of the Muslims were condemning him. I said, "This brother is a Muslim, and I don't care what he's done or what he's been accused of—if he believes in Allah and performs the salat, then I'm with him even if the whole world is against him." Things quieted down after that, and eventually most of the Muslims took my position. But I know that my reputation suffered among the non-Muslims and even among some of the Muslims. I was willing to accept that because I had realized that the pleasure of Allah is greater than seeking the favor of the people. This was the lesson of Noah, who did the right thing even though it was unpopular among his people. As the Qur'an says, "The Guidance of Allah—that is the only guidance."

Finding a Producer

RIGHT AFTER I HAD RECORDED "Round My Way" with DJ Dezerk in May 2019, I was talking to my friend Brendan Vick and asked him if he knew any producers. He mentioned Travis Cherry. Travis was from Raleigh and he and my brother used to hang out, but he was now a big-time producer in Atlanta. I figured that Travis wouldn't have time for me, but Brendan insisted. "Rome, you really need to holler at Travis," he said. As it turns out, when my sister created a Facebook page for me, Travis Cherry was on my friend list. I was surprised. This important producer in Atlanta had friended me on Facebook? I asked my wife to contact him and tell him about my situation. He responded immediately and sent his personal phone number. I called him right away, and to my surprise he was happy to hear from me. I told him about my SoundCloud page and that I had recently recorded a song with DJ Dezerk that I believed was gonna be a Raleigh hood anthem. We talked a few more times and developed a friendship. Travis told me that I didn't have to abandon my pursuit of recording quality music. He related how he had done a song for Bone Thugs-N-Harmony and had recorded one of the group's rappers—Flesh-n-Bone—over the phone when he was in prison. Travis played the track for me, and I honestly couldn't tell which vocals were Flesh's in terms of sound quality. My hope was restored. I said to myself, this can be done.

And then in August 2019, I saw an article in the local Raleigh newspaper that caught my attention. It was called "Next Level Hip Hop," and it was about a new summer program at UNC–Chapel Hill called the Carolina Hip Hop Institute run by a music professor named Mark Katz. He's now my friend and my coauthor, but at the time I had no idea who he was. I decided to write to him—just like I'd written to a lot of other people—in the hope that he could help me. "I know my situation may seem despairing and perhaps unlike anyone you've worked with before," I wrote, "but despite the circumstances, I still have faith and I still have a dream, and I believe that with the right sound and someone who knows what to do with my vocals I can accomplish something BIG!"

I didn't hear from him for almost two months, but when he wrote back, he said he had listened to my music and would see if he could find a producer to work with me. He also said he didn't think it would be a bad thing if my vocals sounded like I was rapping into a phone because it had a distinctive quality that reflected my circumstances. I responded immediately. "Yes, PLEASE PLEASE PLEASE connect me with some producers who would be happy to provide some beats for me!!! I cannot tell you enough how much I would appreciate that. I agree with you about the sound quality. It gives it grit and realness. I feel like that is missing so much in music nowadays. Everything is so polished and shiny and computer generated with perfect timing and my soul is craving for that RAW, straight from the beat box/turntable style hip hop." I didn't hide my feelings. "I'm like a starving dog hungry for a scrap," I wrote. "I'm like literally pacing the cell trying to find a way to do this music just to get it out of my soul, just to say what I've been dying to say for years. Just to be heard."

Katz then connected me to Nick Low-Beer, a producer who lives in New York whose artist name is Nick Neutronz. By January 2020, we were recording songs, with me rapping on the phone and him putting a beat to it. He was genuinely excited about the project and said that I was a "seasoned veteran and a master of my craft." He told me he would try to get the best sound possible, but a lot of it would hinge on the listener. He said that once people heard my story they would be interested in the music. I understood his point, but naturally as an artist I want people to like my music because it's good and not just because of my circumstances. That's the goal. Of course, if I need my story to get their attention, then that's a means to an end.

It was amazing to hear myself rapping to a beat when Nick would play back for me what he had created. I could never hear it like he did because he has a real studio and I just have the prison phone. I'm sure I miss a lot of nuances, but it's good enough for me to know whether I like the sound and to give Nick feedback. For example, the beat he made for "All I Know . . ." was BANANAS. When I listened to the instrumental it evoked so much color. I was visualizing zebras and peacocks and waterfalls. I know that might sound crazy, but I could feel this jungle vibe and when I tried rapping my lyrics over it, I was like "Uhhhh!" It felt so savage and it fit the madness and mayhem that I was trying to describe in the lyrics. The weird thing is that I wrote the lyrics more than fifteen years before I heard Nick's beat, and I never had that type of sound in mind when I wrote it.

I've now been working with Nick for four years. He's my dude. He believes in what I'm doing. He takes my suggestions and he's all in on creating something new and innovative with me. I told him we are gonna create a new sound and make the listeners love it. I have so much inside of me that I've been waiting years to get out. A lot of my songs deal with race and social injustice, but nobody wanted to hear those messages twenty years ago. It's like Allah preserved everything I wrote for the right season, and finally, the season has arrived.

He Doesn't Deserve to Be Here

SABUR ISN'T THAT VOCAL or expressive unless you really get to know him. This is because he has a speech impediment. He stutters. We bonded over music and our friendship grew from that. He talks to me, but not that much to anybody else. On top of that, the dude is greener than an ecologist. It's funny to me sometimes because his innocence sticks out awkwardly. There's no way I could capture his full story, his character, who he is. What I tell you will probably sound too good to be true, but I promise that if you ever get a chance to know him you will agree that my descriptions don't do him justice. He's a genuinely good dude.

One time he told me about how he used to visit this old folks' home every weekend. He first went there with a friend who was visiting a relative and just loved sitting and listening to the residents talk. He started visiting on his own and developed genuine relationships with some of the residents. He would spend his whole day listening to their stories. I asked him why, and he said he just enjoyed it. To him it was no big deal. Sometimes he'd pick up all the neighborhood kids and take them to the park, buy them hot dogs and ice cream. I'd never done anything like that. None of the people I hung out with were visiting old folks and taking kids to the park. My stories from the street are filled with crime and decadence. Sabur doesn't have stories like that. The dude is actually a good guy, which is almost unheard-of in this place. But he doesn't even see any of those things as good or special. It's just what he liked doing. Imagine some of our conversations. I'm giving him the play-by-play of some war story and he's listening with wide-eyed amazement, soaking it all in. When I finish, he says he feels like he was at the movies and he tells me something like, "Man, you are a wild dude. I can't imagine doing all that stuff. Weren't you afraid?" And I'm looking at him like, "What? Afraid?" *Doesn't he realize we are at ground zero for Super Macho Thug Life Gangsta Gangsta Criminals? Even if I was afraid, the code dictates posturing. Doesn't he know the CODE?* Apparently not. This is just a casual example of what I mean when I say he doesn't deserve to be here.

Let me tell you about Sabur's case. He and his girlfriend were at home together in a trailer they shared. Sabur said he was in the kitchen, and she went to light the kerosene heater. Moments later he said she came running into the living room screaming and on fire. He said he ran to her aid. Pushed her out the front door and began rolling her in the grass trying to put her out. He suffered some burns to the back of his hands. After putting out the fire, he picked her up and brought her in the house. Seeing how severely she was burned, he turned on the shower and wet several towels and wrapped her up. They didn't have a telephone, and he told her he was going to get help. But she begged him not to leave her and said she didn't want to go the hospital. She was afraid and probably in shock. I can only imagine how traumatized I might be after seeing the permanent disfigurement of my body and face, knowing that it could never be reversed. I think she didn't want to be alone. He decided to get help, but when he returned to the trailer, he couldn't find her. He later found her hiding in the closet, afraid of going to the hospital. Finally, her family came over, and after her sister saw how badly she was burned, she went to get medical help. Those who stayed behind wanted to know what happened. Despite being told by both Sabur and his girlfriend that she caught fire trying to light the heater, I don't think they wanted to believe that. I think they suspected foul play. But Sabur had absolutely nothing to do with the fire. When the ambulance arrived, his girlfriend even asked him to ride with her to the hospital, which he did. Upon arrival, and before any sedation, the nurse asked her if someone had done this to her, and she responded no several times. She was coherent and aware. She was then transferred to a burn center and questioned several times en route if Sabur had done this to her. Each time she said no in the presence of EMT staff.

After almost two weeks her condition worsened. She developed sepsis and was heavily medicated, unable to talk. Two detectives came to question her with the help of a nurse. She was only able to respond by nodding or shaking her head. According to their testimony, she was asked if Stacey (Sabur's government name) had done this to her, and she shook her head no. Then she was told that Stacey had been arrested and was no longer a threat to her. They said that their clothes were being tested and wanted to know if they had gotten into a fight earlier that day. They said she nodded yes. Then they asked if Stacey had poured gas on her and lit a match. And they said that she nodded her head yes. Hours later, she died. There are numerous questions about her competency at the time she was questioned. Was she disoriented and confused? She was on a continuous fentanyl drip for pain and had received sedatives earlier that day. Yet that final nod of the head sealed Sabur's fate.

He swears he didn't set her on fire. He honestly doesn't know what happened. But the State had a few witnesses who testified that Sabur and his girlfriend had been fighting earlier that day. Sabur said that was untrue. I believe him without reservation. I mean, if he set her on fire in the first place, why would he put the fire out and save her life? If he did that, wouldn't he know that she was gonna tell them he did it? It would make more sense to just let her die and blame it on the heater exploding. But he tried to save her. He wrapped her in wet towels and sought help. She asked for him to ride in the ambulance with her. Not her sister or anyone else. And she denied that he had anything to do with this for as long as she could talk and was coherent.

Sabur's not supposed to be here, and he's been locked up for thirty years. It's a shame. I don't know what to do and he doesn't either. He's probably written to every organization that represents innocent people. And he's gotten to the point where even though he won't say it, it seems like he's given up hope. The system has obviously failed him, and his attorneys haven't been pushing for him to be released. I can't imagine what it's like. I've told him before that although I wish I was innocent because I could hold on to that as hope that one day I might get out, I don't know if I could bear the burden of being here for all these years knowing that I never committed a crime.

One Life

You ever wished you could change an injustice?
Correct a wrong that's a shame and disgustin'
Remove pain of someone achin' and sufferin'
Now is the time we gotta rise with a purpose
We got to lend a hand
To save the whole world's like saving one man
Do everything you can and let the whole world know
How Stacey Tyler was sentenced to Death Row
1993 was the year
He was at home with just his girlfriend there
She was on the sofa while he was in the kitchen
Since it was November the temperature was frigid
She said it was chilly as he opened up the freezer
He said if you're cold then baby go light up the heater

Thirty seconds later she was screamin' out his name
Shocked when he looked up her hair and shoulders were in
 flames

I'ma let the whole world know
An innocent man is locked up on Death Row
We can do something we can make things right
To save the whole world is to save one life

So he rushed over to her and extinguished the flames
Nursed her wounds until the ambulance came
By then her mother, sister and her daughter was there
The sight of her burns really had all of 'em scared
She spoke softly as she told the EMT
In the ambulance, I want Stacey to ride with me
He rode in the van to the hospital
Hoping a good outcome was possible
When they arrived, they rushed her to the Trauma Unit
Then the cops came to ask Stacey did he do it?
Shocked, but of course he denied he did
But for hours the police implied he did
On the other side the hospital staff was askin'
His girlfriend if she could explain how this happened
She told them before they sedated her
Stacey did not set the blaze to her

I'ma let the whole world know
An innocent man is locked up on Death Row
We can do something we can make this right
To save the whole world is to save one life

In the burn center his girl struggled for two weeks
Her health got worse she wasn't able to speak
They kept her sedated to protect from pain
But on the day of her death two detectives came
They claim in the moments before her last breath
When asked if he did it she nodded her head yes
When thirty seconds prior she had shook her head no
But a confused nod sent Stacey to Death Row

Alim Braxton (*right*) and Sabur Tyler (*left*).
Drawing by Cerron T. Hooks.

With low funds his legal defense was so shoddy
All that he knew was he NEVER killed nobody
No motive and no reason why he'd hurt her
Still found guilty of first-degree murder
You ever wished you could change an injustice?
Correct a wrong that's a shame and disgustin'
Remove pain of someone achin' and sufferin'
Now is the time we gotta rise with a purpose
We got to lend a hand
To save the whole world's like saving one man
Do everything you can and let the whole world know
How Stacey Tyler was sentenced to Death Row

I'ma let the whole world know
An innocent man is locked up on Death Row
We can do something we can make this right
To save the whole world is to save one life

Dreamville and the Nightmare

N 2019, J. COLE, North Carolina's most famous rapper, held his first Dreamville Festival at Dorothea Dix Park, literally across the street from Central Prison. We could hear the music thumping through our walls. Me and Sabur talked about it. Forty thousand people there and probably not one had a clue that right across the street was Death Row. There we were, locked up, hidden behind walls. I told Sabur that across the street from Dreamville he was living the Nightmare. And I vowed that one day they were going to be saying our names from that Dreamville stage. I am determined to let the world know of his innocence. I think of my song "Unbreakable," where I say:

> I cannot turn a blind eye and just act like everything's pretty
> When we got people on Death Row right here in the heart of
>   the city
> And that's real life, no make-believe and no Hollywood . . .

If I had the chance to talk to J. Cole, here's what I would say: I love what you have done by bringing the Dreamville Festival to Raleigh and making it an annual event. I love this city and this state, and my heart swells with pride to see one of its native sons put on for North Carolina like you are. If I could ask one thing, it would be to use your platform and your voice to bring attention to the fact that Stacey Tyler and Elrico Fowler are two innocent men literally right across the street from Dreamville. They have been languishing on Death Row for decades for crimes they did not commit. They don't have a voice or any exceptional talent to bring attention to their cases, and nobody even knows they are here. But if you could just say their names, then the city, the media, the people will hear you and the process of getting them justice can begin. I'm not asking you to vouch for them. I'm not asking you to believe without investigating their claims. I just ask that you say their names and let the world know that they are here. I have faith that Allah will do the rest.

What's the Point in Trying to Do Good?

VERY ONCE IN A WHILE, I have a conversation with a friend in here that leaves my heart heavy. A while back I had to tell my friend the kind of truth that can crush hopes to powder. Basically, the conversation involved his false hope of getting out of here. I'm talking about a man who killed three people when he was nineteen during a home invasion. He was telling me about some letters and articles he had written to drum up support for those who commit serious crimes under the age of twenty-one. He said there was science that showed that the brain was still growing at that age, and the courts had ruled that it was unconstitutional to sentence people under eighteen to life without parole on the same grounds. He felt that with enough attention brought to the science of adolescent brains the court would expand the ruling to those twenty-one and under.

I understood. I knew what was going on. He was trying to figure out a way to get up out of here. I get it. I want to go home, too. But I asked him if a nineteen-year-old killed his mother the exact same way he committed his crime, should the murderer get a second chance because his brain wasn't fully developed? This is what started the conversation.

He asked me what he could do to bring attention to his case. "How am I supposed to show people that I'm rehabilitated?" he asked. I said, "Well, is what you doing just for show?" "Naw," he said, "it's science." "Well, if it's science," I responded, "then you just have to continue to do the work." I said anytime people do something to get our attention, we doubt their sincerity. That's just a natural response. The people who are really sincere just keep doing what they are doing, and sometimes other people see them and sometimes they don't.

I told him that's why the spiritual path is so hard. Because the believer doesn't do things for the acknowledgment of the world or for others to see. He does it to please his Lord. If his Lord is pleased and wants to honor and reward him in this life, then He may reward him. But if He chooses to reward him in the next life, he must be content with it as long as his Lord is pleased.

My friend looked despondent. "What's the point in trying to do good?" he asked. "It's too hard, and it's no fun. I just feel like saying fuck it. Fuck everything. I'm just too impatient." Again, I understood. I told him that there is a hadith that the Muslims have that says, "This world is a prison for the believers and paradise for the disbelievers." It's hard doing the right thing. The people doing the wrong things are having all the fun. It's easy to fall into despair and become hopeless, but that's a dark and dangerous place. Next thing you know, you don't care about nothing no more, including taking someone's life.

This is the real stuff that people in here struggle with. It's like I said in a bar from one of my songs: "I'm speakin' for those that's in the system, innocent but can't get no assistance / and those who wanna do right but can't get no redemption."

Hoops and Obstacles

EVEN THOUGH I NOW had a producer, it seemed like every obstacle that could arise sprung up and multiplied. At times I was so discouraged, I believed that this was not meant to be, that Allah did not want me to do this. Sabur said, "But how do you know"? "Sabur," I answered, "if Allah doesn't want this to happen, there's nothing in the universe that can cause it to happen." But then he made a good point: "If your solution to everything that doesn't go the way you planned is that it wasn't the will of Allah, then you can always use that as an excuse for giving up."

It really got intense one time when I told him I couldn't do it anymore. "What if it's just a fantasy and I'm wasting my life away dreaming about something that will never be? Isn't it better to let that dream go and deal with the reality in front of me? I mean, get real. We're on Death Row and I'm talking about being a rapper! Is it foolish?" He looked at me, and I'll never forget what he said. He had tears in his eyes. "Let me tell you something," he said.

Art by Cerron Hooks featuring Sabur Tyler and the
names of formerly or currently incarcerated people
on Death Row who have been exonerated or who
have innocence claims.

"The thing I admire about you is that you still have the ability to dream. I'm
innocent. But they took that from me. I don't even know how to dream no
more. I've got to latch myself on to your dream and that's the only thing I've
got left. I believe in this shit more than any other dream that I've had. And if
you talking 'bout how you can just walk away without seeing what happens
just because things aren't going according to your timetable, then you aren't
just giving up on your dream, but on mine too. And it's the only one I've got
left." Talk about a deep conversation. After that, we sat there for a while in
his cell and I said, "Man, who's gonna believe this shit? If we actually make
it, who's gonna believe everything that we've been through?" He said, "Man,
you can't make this shit up!"

But by the end of January 2020, I had recorded vocals for seventeen songs.
It had been so hard, and so much work just to get that far. After all the hoops

and obstacles I had to jump through and overcome just to record my voice, I felt like I had really achieved something. But I was just getting started.

A few months later I was leaving the chow hall after lunch when two COs from the SRG (Security Risk Group) Division of Internal Affairs approached me. One said, "I'm gonna be straight up with you. You're recording music, right?" I said, "Yeah." He asked me, "How are you doing it?" I said, "Over the phone." They said, "Okay. Well, keep doing what you're doing." "Have y'all heard some of my stuff?" I asked. They got all excited. "Yeah, we've heard your stuff. 'Original Gangster.' 'One War.' You got flow, too. It's tight." I smiled and thanked them. I felt pretty good walking back to the unit. The whole vibe reminded me of the closing scene from *Hustle and Flow*, one of my favorite movies. The main character DJay is being escorted to his prison cell when the two COs say they heard his song on the radio. Turns out they're fans of his and aspiring rappers. One even hands DJay a demo tape! I was glad that the administration knew about my music, and at the time I assumed they had no qualms with it other than wanting to know how I was recording it.

Why Rappers Should Listen to Country Music

SEVERAL YEARS AGO, around 2009, I felt totally uninspired by hip hop. Most of the songs I heard on the radio were formulaic. They fit a similar structure and were all about the same things: money, women, cars, fashion, bravado, gunplay, and drugs. I was hungry for something more fulfilling. So one night I turned my radio dial past the hip hop station. I listened to some rock, but nothing grabbed my attention. Then I turned to the country station and the first song I heard was "Watching You" by Rodney Atkins. It tells the story of a man who just left MacDonald's after buying his four-year-old son a Happy Meal. They're driving through town when the man has to slam on his brakes, spilling the boy's drink. The dad is shocked when the boy says a four-letter word and asks him where he learned to talk like that. The boy says, "I've been watching you, Dad, ain't that cool / I'm your buckaroo, I wanna be like you." This becomes the chorus of the song. That night before bed the man goes to his son's room and finds him on his knees praying. He asks his son where he learned to pray like that, and the boy says, "I've been watching you, Dad, ain't that cool / I'm your buckaroo, I wanna be like you." Man, what a beautiful song, so full of meaning. It made the hairs on my neck stand up.

What have I been missing? I thought. I listened to the next song and the next and each one was something new and different. There were songs about love, hope, family, God, country, and so much more. I fell in love with the music and listened to nothing but country for about four years straight after that. Some of my favorites are "You're Gonna Miss This" by Trace Atkins, and "Lucky Man" and "Something to Be Proud Of" by Montgomery Gentry. I like Taylor Swift and Carrie Underwood, Garth Brooks, Toby Keith, Tim McGraw, Reba McIntire, and more. I turned a lot of guys on the Row to country who are still big fans now.

It's crazy because my grandma used to LOVE country music! When I was fifteen and was kicked out of Wake County schools for calling in a bomb threat as a prank, my mom sent me to her little hometown of Ayden, in Pitt County, to live with my grandma. I remember my grandma had one of those little alarm clock radios in the kitchen, and she would have country music on all day. It drove me crazy. I was a hip hop head who was all about bass and rap—all I could hear was that fiddle and the other country instruments and I thought it sucked! But when I started listening to country music years later, that sound made me nostalgic for the days I stayed with my grandma. Every weekday she and I would eat a TV dinner that the Meals on Wheels people brought around and watch the sitcom *Night Court* together.

I aspire to write the type of songs that I hear country artists sing. Take "Lucky Man" by Montgomery Gentry. The song starts, "I have days where I hate my job / This little town and the whole world too." But then he talks about all the things he has—a family, a house, a truck, a little bit of money, and his health—and realizes that he truly is a lucky man. Just imagine if more rappers developed that type of humility and gratitude for the blessings in their life despite the hardships. A song like "Lucky Man" will still be relevant in fifty years, but most of the big hip hop songs won't be played three to five years from now.

I'm not the first one to complain about the lack of substance in rap. KRS-One talked about this back in 1988 in the Boogie Down Productions song "My Philosophy." He says, "Some MCs be talkin' and talkin'/ Tryin' to show

how Black people are walkin'," but those rappers lack creativity and just re-inforce negative stereotypes. Of course, there may be hip hop songs out there like "Lucky Man" in spirit, but they aren't the most popular ones, and that's not what I hear on the radio in Central Prison. I want to write hip hop songs that move you emotionally. That touch your heart, make you appreciate your family, give you pride in your accomplishments, even make you cry.

My Baby Sister Keisha

'VE READ ABOUT ARTISTS and their struggles. Those who succeed have usually trodden an arduous path filled with setbacks and disappointments. It makes you appreciate their success even more. I get all that, in theory. But there are some setbacks you don't recover from.

I'll never forget February 5, 2020. Things had been going well. I was recording songs with Nick and was excited about my progress. I was writing a letter in my cell that day when the sergeant told me that my mother needed to talk to me. When I called, she told me that my baby sister Keisha had had a heart attack. My mom was crying and urged me to pray for Keisha.

I found out later that Keisha's boyfriend, who works third shift, came home and found her on the couch at about 7 a.m. She didn't have a pulse and wasn't breathing. He called the paramedics and when they arrived, they performed CPR and were eventually able to get a weak pulse. They transported her to the hospital in Kenansville, NC, and called my mom. My mom called

Undated photo of Keisha Braxton.
Courtesy of Marie Braxton.

my brother Chris and his wife, Quita, and they picked my mom up and drove to the hospital. When they arrived my sister was on life support and that's around the time I spoke to my mom. She was on life support for five days, but she never showed any brain activity. The doctors said that the only thing that kept her breathing was the machine. So we decided to pull the plug. My mother lost her baby girl. My nephew lost his mom. I lost my sister.

For days afterward I didn't have the energy or focus to do anything. I cried every day. I cried just thinking about her voice. We were so close. My family was super, super tight-knit. When I say family, I mean me, my mom, my brother Chris, and my sister Keisha. We were all we had for so many years. There was nobody else but us. That's why it's so hard. I talked to Keisha every week. I still miss her so much.

Keisha was one of my biggest fans. Before she died, she told my mom that she loved the songs I had just recorded. Right before they took her off life support, my mom, my brother Chris, and my stepdad Jesse gathered around her in a circle, holding hands. Then Chris played one of my songs for her on his phone, the one she liked best. It's called "Land of the Profits." I was incredibly honored that they played my song for her at the hospital. It broke my heart when my mom recounted the story to me. She said Chris put the phone up by her head and said, "Lucy, go on and ride to this." Lucy was a nickname I gave her when she was a little girl.

Keisha believed in me so much that she told my mom and my brother Chris that she wanted to start a record label just for my music. She was one of the first people to hear the songs I did with Nick Neutronz. After she heard "Land of the Profits," she told me, "That joint right there is fire. I can bop to this!" She died a couple weeks later.

June 10 is Keisha's birthday. On the first birthday after she passed, I ate butter pecan ice cream in her honor because it was her favorite. She even had a tattoo on her upper arm that said, "Butter Pecan." She would've been forty-three. I sure wish she could see what I've done with my music. I know she would be so proud. But I'm glad she got to hear at least one of my songs and could see how far I'd come.

Almost Like She Was in Paradise

HAD MY FIRST-EVER VIDEO VISIT on May 17, 2020. I was taken to a cubicle where they had a laptop set up, and I was able to talk with my mom for fifteen minutes. It was out of this world! It's no big deal to people who do this every day, but it was a big deal for me. I had never talked on a cell phone before, never been on the internet, never video chatted. So that was one thing, the novelty of it all. But the most amazing aspect was seeing my mom *at home*. She was sitting on the couch in the living room like it was the most normal thing. Something that she does every single day. But I was in awe. Every time I had seen her for the previous twenty-seven years, I'd seen her in the exact same place, with the same concrete walls, the same off-white paint, the bars that refuse me an unobscured look at her face. The same floors, the same steel, the same scratches and smudges on the windows. To see her in a setting other than a prison visiting booth made it look almost like she was in paradise. The couch looked so comfortable, and she was relaxed. It broke my heart to know that for all those years she would leave that comfort to come and sit with me for two hours each week in a cramped booth.

Then my mom took me for a tour around the house. She showed me the living room, her furniture, the pictures on the wall, the colors of the walls, the carpet. Then we went into the kitchen. She had hardwood floors, and the countertops looked like marble. I saw the dishwasher and the refrigerator and the stove. A coffeepot. Three pears on the counter. I saw upstairs, including my old bedroom and my sister's old bedroom. I saw the urn with Keisha's ashes. My nephew, Keisha's son, was there that day too, so I saw him. My eyes soaked up every detail.

Then she went to the front door and said, "Let me show you my flowers." When she opened the door, I swear I cringed because I thought we were going to get in trouble. I wanted to say, "Mom, we can't go outside!" I've been conditioned to think like a prisoner and going outside without permission is not allowed. But she opened the door, not having a clue of my worries, and stepped right outside and showed me her flowers. I had to smile. Man, I've forgotten what it's like to feel free. How many people take the time to even recognize the freedom they have? I told my mom it was like going on a field trip!

Waking Up in a Different Country

ON SUNDAY, MAY 31, 2020, six days after the murder of George Floyd, I woke up in a different country. Gil Scott-Heron had said that "The Revolution Will Not Be Televised," but as I stayed up into the late hours of the night watching the protests from Death Row, all I could think was that the Revolution *is* being televised! I watched with pride and excitement as a thousand people—and so many Black people—were making their voices be heard in *my city*, the capital of North Carolina. Raleigh is a city that I feel doesn't get enough respect. We don't have the rich history of Black communities in cities like Durham, which was once known as Black Wall Street, or Greensboro, connected to the birth of the civil rights movement with the sit-ins at the segregated Woolworth's. So I was surprised and proud to see my city take a stand.

As the hours passed and nightfall came, things got more aggressive. I saw windows being broken, stores being broken into, and fires being started. I thought to myself, *Why are they doing this?* I felt like these were some ignorant muthafuckas, possibly gangbangers and rowdy street niggas just looking to fuck shit up. Niggas acting like niggas. The first chance we get to make a stance, to let our voice be heard, we do some old rachet-ass dumb shit to make us look like a bunch of thugs and criminals. I saw graffiti being sprayed on buildings—stuff like "BLM," "ACAB," "Fuck 12"—and in my ignorance I thought these were gang tags. I was heartbroken that my people would take such a righteous cause and turn it into gang graffiti.

I found myself wondering, *What are white people gonna think? They are gonna frown and say we are just a bunch of hoodlums.* I imagined some of them saying, "I'm outraged at the sight of a white police officer kneeling on the neck of George Floyd, but why are you destroying my property? Why are you busting out my windows?"

I worried that this was only going to fuel racism. Whites would become more suspicious and distrustful of Blacks. They would say, "I can't trust you people. I've lived among you, employed you, provided you with service, and this is how you repay me? You destroy my property." I imagined, in the aftermath, that whites would become more supportive of the police and more suspicious of Blacks. Blacks would, in turn, feel that mistrust and harsh treatment and display it by being visibly hostile, angry, and rude. The two sides would just feed on each's hatred.

The next day I spoke to a few others to hear their perspective. I learned that BLM stood for Black Lives Matter, and that ACAB meant All Cops Are Bastards, and that 12 stood for the police. These weren't gang tags at all. They were statements of protest written on the walls. I asked a guy from my city what he thought. He said he liked what the protesters did. But, I asked, how were white people gonna feel about that, especially business owners whose property was destroyed? He said it was too late to worry about all that—it was finally time for action. "We've been too busy worrying about what others are gonna think, and the same shit keeps happening over and over. We're finally saying enough is enough and you are gonna feel this too."

That had a heavy impact on me. I retreated into myself and began sorting out all the voices. I realized that most of the criticism of the protesters was coming from people on the sidelines, or from the establishment. People more concerned with preserving the present order, even at the cost of injustice. How were these people entitled to define what protest looked like? I realized that even within myself I had begun to espouse the sentiments of those in power. I had to check myself hard. The struggle, the fight, the protest is against the established order. Yet I realized that it was the police that were trying to tell people how they should protest. It was the media that was characterizing the protest as rioting and looting and violent and unacceptable. It was politicians who were saying that we need to take our voices to the ballot box because that's where change comes from. And it was even some middle-class Blacks who didn't want to rock the boat, who would rather endure slights and injustices as long as it wasn't one of their loved ones killed by the police.

I started remembering history. I remembered that at the dawn of the civil rights movement, it was the older generation that was opposed to sit-ins and freedom rides and protest. They were more concerned with preserving a measure of peace and security. Sure, there was segregation and discrimination, but they didn't want to take a step backward. Things were better than they once were. I felt like I was seeing the same history being replayed.

The establishment can't tell the oppressed what is acceptable. The people you are protesting against can't tell you how to go about it. I mean, we've marched already. We've held hands. We've cried. We've picketed. We've assembled peacefully over and over and over. And what has changed? Nothing. The police ain't changing. I thought to myself that even if they crucified Derek Chauvin, it wasn't gonna change the police treatment of Black people. So what if we have Black police chiefs and sheriffs and even a Black president? That didn't stop white cops from killing unarmed Black people. They can't tell us that voting is the answer.

I realized that something was happening. Something like I'd never witnessed in my lifetime. The cause is righteous. It's just. Who am I to criticize those out there doing something to change it? I don't know how this thing is gonna unfold, but I'm supporting the cause. I actually wrote a song a few years ago called "White Cop," and unfortunately it's still relevant today.

Almost a year later, on April 20, 2021, Derek Chauvin was convicted on all counts. It felt like a victory, and I even shed a tear. This was a change from all the previous acquittals of cops who murdered unarmed Black people and all the times cops never even got charged. From Rodney King to Breonna Taylor. I felt a sense of vindication, even pride, like America had come together to do the right thing. It was one of only two times I ever felt proud of America. The other time was when Barack Obama was elected president.

But in the same breath, I felt sorry for Chauvin because he was a sacrificial lamb. I watched on TV as he stood up and put his hands behind his back and did his best to maintain his composure while the entire world came down on his head. I knew how he'd feel when that cell door closed and he would be alone with nothing but his thoughts. He probably felt betrayed and abandoned, and he probably didn't believe he did anything wrong. I imagine that in his mind he believed that he never intended to kill George Floyd, that at worst it was an accident. I think his pride and ego got in the way and he didn't want to give in to the demands of the crowd. I think his refusal to remove his knee from George Floyd's neck was his way of saying to the crowd that he was the one in control. And I don't think that he believed his actions would result in George Floyd's death. For all those reasons I actually felt sorry for him. But the angry part of me didn't care. The angry part of me wanted somebody to pay, not just for George Floyd, but also for Amadou Diallo, Eric Garner, Philando Castille, and the countless others who've died at the hands of police. That's the consequence of injustice. If you do injustice to me for so long, I feel a sense of vindication even if the same injustice happens to you. But what kind of system is that? As Childish Gambino said: This is America.

White Cop

White Cop! White Cop, White Cop, White Cop
Your shooting Black people has got to stop
The slightest altercation and your gun goes Pop!
Every few months another body gets dropped
"Hands up, don't shoot," and we still get shot
Take your 9 mil and take it off cock
Take your .45 and put it 'pon lock
White Cop, White Cop

Bo! Bo! Bo! That's the sound of the police
(Damn) another Blackman deceased
Killed in the streets
The racial violence don't cease
Year after year, the cycle repeats and repeats, and repeats

Officer shoots Blackman, officer kills Blackman
This happens over and over and over
From Baton Rouge to Minnesota
Black men gunned down by another white patroller
We march for justice but get nothin'
We cry and pray and protect and keep struggling
Even appeal to the government
Hoping that they will prosecute
The guilty cops that shoot
But they all get acquittals
You think Black lives matter? Black lives mean little
And they justify it by sayin' we're violent so their protection
    must be due
But white cop if you were put here to protect us, then who
    protects us from you?

White Cop! White Cop, White Cop, White Cop
Your shooting Black people has got to stop
The slightest altercation and your gun goes Pop!
Every few months another body gets dropped
"Hands up, don't shoot," and we still get shot
Take your 9 mil and take it off cock
Take your .45 and put it 'pon lock
White Cop, White Cop

Here's what the East and the West have in common
They both have white cops who be racial profiling
Young Black kids in the West have stress
In the East we are killed by the same white police
Not every white cop is a murderer
Some will sacrifice their life protecting and serving ya
But a few are quite homicidal, haven't you heard?
It was white cops killing Blacks in Charleston and Ferguson
Enough white cop, that's enough, with every injustice
We are getting more disgusted
We're teaching our kids to obey, we comply with your orders
    and we still get slaughtered
But this is the hypocrisy

If it was Black cops killing white kids this would not just be
'Cause the government would make it stop
Or every white American would want to kill that Black cop!

White Cop! White Cop, White Cop, White Cop
Your shooting Black people has got to stop
The slightest altercation and your gun goes Pop!
Every few months another body gets dropped
"Hands up, don't shoot," and we still get shot
Take your 9 mil and take it off cock
Take your .45 and put it 'pon lock
White Cop, White Cop

A hundred years ago Blacks were killed by white cops
They never stood trial or even lost their jobs
Recently on TV you see the same white cop
The same mind state but just a different mugshot
They tell us be patient while we facin' gunshots
A hundred years of patience still the killing ain't stopped
A hundred years of lynchin' did I mention, white cop
You just get a paid suspension wit' your missus, white cop
You don't even go to prison for these killings, white cop
A hundred years of lynchin' did I mention?
White Cop, White Cop, White Cop
It's white on Black violence again nonstop!

Welcome Back to Unit One

ONE DAY IN EARLY June 2020 I was writing a letter during count time when my cell door suddenly opened. The officer in the booth told me to go to the sergeant's office. They rarely open cell doors during count, so I was wondering if I was about to receive some bad news. When I got word of Keisha's death it was the same thing. This time, when I got to the office the sergeant stood up and looked me in the eye and said, "I just got a call from the captain down at Master Control and they told us that we have to lock you up." This is what they say at Central Prison when they put you in segregation, or solitary confinement. "We don't know why, but somebody from Internal Affairs will talk to you tomorrow." I just nodded my head. Even though I wasn't expecting it, and knew I hadn't done anything wrong, I also knew that there was nothing I could say or do to prevent what was about to happen. I was fuming but I did my best to appear composed. My mind was racing. What was this about?

I wondered if it was connected with my music. Maybe my recording of "White Cop" went viral and this was an attempt to silence me. As far as my music is concerned that's always a possibility. Me and Sabur had talked about it numerous times. But I've always been willing to sacrifice whatever is necessary to get this music out because it's so much bigger than me. In here, you can never take anything for granted. Even though I wasn't breaking any rules, I was doing something unprecedented. The system doesn't necessarily like unprecedented, and I knew that they could shut me down at any time. That's why I wanted to get the work out and in the hands of other people so it could keep moving forward. By the grace of Allah, I had managed to record over twenty songs by that time, about fifteen of them with my producer Nick Neutronz. So at least the work was preserved. I still had more to record but even if I never said another word I'd said enough to be heard.

They put me in a filthy cell. The back wall had a picture of a human skull drawn on it from floor to ceiling. All I had at that time was the clothes on my back and an ink pen in my pocket. They brought me a food tray and it had a pack of peanut butter on it, the only thing I figured I could sell so I could get a stamp to write a letter. Nobody is gonna buy collard greens, boiled potatoes, or applesauce. I asked the janitor if he had a stamp. I told him all I had was a pack of peanut butter but I would pay him more later. He gave me a stamp and I gave him the peanut butter. About four hours later, they brought a few items from my personal property including some food. Food items from the canteen are a hot commodity on lock-up. So I gave the janitor a pack of mackerel (valued at $1.75) for two more stamps. I'm sure he would've paid more if I'd asked, but I was showing my gratitude for giving me that first stamp for only a pack of peanut butter (worth about twenty cents).

They ended up moving me to another cell because I have sleep apnea and I use a CPAP machine, so I need to be close to a wall socket. It was cleaner than the other cell, but still nasty. They gave me a blanket, two sheets and a towel and washcloth. I ripped the towel in half and wet it and did my best to scrub the floor. It was filthy. But I have to pray, so I scrubbed the floor the best I could. Apparently an artist had been in here. The walls were covered with the words PEACE, HOPE and LOVE with hearts and peace signs and a cross. Everything was done in color too: pink, blue, and yellow. Between a heart and a cross someone had written FUCK 12 in ink. There was a pentagram and a circle and the words "Nether Light" above it. To the right was another circle with a five-point star in it and the image of a man with his arms extended to each side. Above it was the word "NorLord." And beneath these two images was a twelve-point star with the words "And Gates Open."

I scrubbed the floor the best I could and made the cell habitable. Apparently there was an artist in here because the walls are covered with the words PEACE, HOPE and LOVE. There's hearts and peace signs and a cross. Everything is done in color too : pink, blue and yellow. Right beside the word Hope and beneath the word Love, between a heart and a cross someone has written FUCK 12 in ink! ☺ (12 is the police by the way). On the wall right in front of me the same artist (I presume) has drawn 3 diagrams in blue. A five-point star with a pentagram and a circle and the word Nether Light above it. Next to it on the right is another circle with a 5 point star in it and the image of a man with his arms extended to each side. Above it is the word NorLord. And beneath these 2 images is a 12 point star with the words: And Gates Open. To the right someone has drawn a makeshift calender. This is what it looks like:

	Rec	Rec		Rec	Rec	Rec
SUN	Mon	Tuesday	Wensday	Thursday	Friday	Saturday
Noting X X ⌒	Outside Rec Showers	Inside Cloths Showers	Noting X X ⌒	Outside Cloths Showers	Inside rec	Inside rec Showers
I aint takin his shit yo mo E B a gangsta	Soap Day Change Boxers	Need Soap Change Boxers	I'm a kill myself	Soap Day Change Boxers		Soap Day Change Boxers

Excerpt, letter from Alim Braxton to Mark Katz, June 22, 2020.

To the right someone had drawn a makeshift calendar. There was a window of opaque glass covered with two metal grates. It's pointless to even call it a window. The only thing you can tell from looking out is if it was night or day.

The next morning they had outside recreation. I don't like the process. They make you strip to your underwear and pass all your clothes out of the food slot in the door. Then they handcuff you behind your back, open the door, and escort you into a holding cell. You are paraded around in your underwear with hands cuffed behind your back. There are female officers walking around. It's humiliating. Besides, they just put you in a small dog cage. They have dozens of them lined up, side by side. The fencing is so dense you can't even see the person in the next cage. So I refused to go outside.

One morning when one of the guys went outside, the sergeant went into his cell. I don't know why. When they brought him back to his cell his mattress was missing. He asked the officers what happened, but they didn't even respond. They closed his door, removed the handcuffs, and left. He started yelling, asking why they took his mattress. He then started yelling for the officer in the control booth to call the sergeant. The officer in the control booth ignored him. So the guy started kicking the cell door. BOOM! BOOM! BOOM! "Call the sergeant!" BOOM! BOOM! BOOM! "Why y'all take my mattress?!" BOOM! BOOM! BOOM! BOOM! BOOM! BOOM! BOOM! BOOM! BOOM! BOOM! After about five minutes the sergeant and another officer came on the block. I heard the guy yell at the sergeant, "How come y'all took my mattress?" The sergeant walked right up to the cell door said, "Shut the fuck up!" Then the other officer opened the trap door and the sergeant pulled out a mini fire hydrant of mace and sprayed his cell with pepper spray. "Now stay the fuck off my door!" the sergeant yelled, and he marched out with the other officer. The guy was coughing so loud that's all you could hear. He couldn't talk.

About ten minutes later, a different sergeant and two other officers came and handcuffed the guy and took him out of the cell. I felt my stomach knot up. I'd seen this happen dozens of times in years past. Usually they'd take him out in the hallway or staircase and then beat him with their batons. He'd come back later with stitches or staples in his head, teeth missing, and body covered in bruises. The officers would claim that he lunged at them or head-butted them and they had to use force to restrain him. I knew the drill. But by the grace of Allah, the next morning the guy came back unharmed. They'd taken him to the nurse who used wet wipes to remove the mace on his body and gave him a clean t-shirt and brought him back to the pepper-sprayed cell. *Welcome back to Unit One*, I thought to myself. Welcome back to Unit One.

Due Process?

I F I WAS INDEED being confined in segregation because of my music or my writings then that is totally political, because I haven't broken any rules in doing what I've done. But when you are in prison, you aren't supposed to be seen. When you are on Death Row you aren't supposed to have a voice. Everyone is considered ignorant. You could be a Harvard graduate, a Rhodes scholar, but if you go to prison, none of your knowledge matters. You could've been a mechanical engineer or a master plumber, and if something breaks down and you try to tell those in charge what the problem is, they will look at you like you are a monkey. What do you know? You're just a stupid inmate. The slave master don't like no smart or uppity niggers.

The first time I heard anything about why I was in segregation was four days after I was locked up. A case manager came to my cell and served me with a Restrictive Housing Interim Procedures form. The only information it gave me was that I was under investigation for an infraction but had not yet been charged. It's like pretrial detainment. The difference is when you are arrested on the street, they at least have to charge you with an offense, whereas in here I hadn't been charged with committing an infraction. No one would even tell me why I was being investigated.

The form had space designated "Offender Response," so this is what I wrote: "I was called to the Sgt.'s office on 6-14-2020 and told that I was being put on lock-up and nobody knows why. I KNOW that I havent broken any rules and nobody has come to explain to me what is going on. I don't know why I am on lock-up when I havent done anything wrong, and it just dont seem fair. At least tell me what it is I am being accused of. This just don't make sense. And why does it take forty-five days to complete an investigation when I havent done NOTHING?!!!" My spelling and wording were deliberate—like I said, inmates are expected to be ignorant.

For a civilian, it is a violation of your civil liberties if the government detains you without charges or without informing you of the reason for detainment. It is a constitutional right for every civilian to be free from any unreasonable searches, seizures, or imprisonment. Although incarcerated people do not enjoy the same protections a free citizen has, the courts have ruled that we have a right to due process. Sure, we can be searched, our property can be seized, and we can be imprisoned in the interests of security. But throwing us in solitary confinement without any explanation is not due process. I'm hammering this home because I want people to know what happens behind these walls. Some will sneer and say we aren't supposed to have rights. We're trash. We don't deserve anything. But we are human, and we deserve basic human rights. The system in this country today is barbaric, inhumane, and, for many of us, an agonizingly slow form of torture.

Celebrating in the Hole

SPENT JULY 4, 2020, in the hole. The holiday never really meant anything to me. When I was on the outside, it meant seeing the fireworks, cooking out. All holidays were just occasions to have fun and celebrate. I didn't pay any real attention to it being Independence Day or what that meant. In here, it used to mean we were served watermelon. That was the only day of the year that we got watermelon. But we haven't gotten watermelon for the last several years. We also used to get a tray with food they cooked on the grill, but we haven't gotten that in years either.

Patriotic holidays have never translated into anything meaningful in my life. I mean, when we talk about *independence*, Black people have never truly experienced independence in this country. True independence is your own land, your own natural resources, wealth, and government. Black people don't have nothing like that. Independence Day is for white people to celebrate. For Black people to feel like Independence Day is theirs, they need to become American first and Black second. But that doesn't translate into reality because everyday life reminds you that you are Black first and American second, third, or fourth. And with that being the reality, what is Independence Day?

The Fourth of July has never been anything for me to celebrate. But about a week later, while I was still in segregation, something truly did bring me joy. It was a letter from my mom. She wrote, "I spent a good part of my morning listening to your music while I watered tomato plants and flowers. Just had my headphones on listening to my son speak his truth." Can you imagine what that meant to me? Tears are streaming down my cheeks right now just thinking about this. There I was in one of the worst situations imaginable, sitting in segregation. I had been away for twenty-seven years. But my mama was at home watering her plants and listening to her son on her headphones, like I was right there. I wasn't supposed to be able to do this. Who could have ever imagined it? I never did. As far as I was concerned, my mission was accomplished. Didn't even matter if nobody else was feeling me. My mom was listening to me on her headphones while she watered her plants. Drop the mic!

Checking In at Central Prison

SPENT SIXTEEN DAYS IN segregation before I was finally told why I was on lock-up. Two officers from Internal Affairs—the same two who had encouraged me to keep making music a few months earlier—came to my cell and told me I was being charged with two offenses, A16 and A99. Here are the descriptions from the official list of Disciplinary Offenses.

(A16) Possess or use in any manner any type of unauthorized recording or image taking device or any type of unauthorized communication device whether audio, video, or data. Examples include but are not limited to cell phones, personal digital assistants, cameras, tape recorders or digital recorders that can be used to send and/or receive any type of messages/images for any purpose.

(A99) Attempt to commit any of the above-listed offenses, aid another person to commit any of the above-listed offenses, or make plans to commit any of the above-mentioned offenses. It shall be no defense that an individual was prevented from completing any of the above offenses by prison staff or intervening circumstances.

I was confused. I didn't have any devices and I wasn't working with anyone using an unauthorized communication device. They clarified and said that I was being charged because someone was posting stuff on social media for me. It couldn't be connected to my SoundCloud page because they already knew about that. Finally, one of them came out and said, "The only reason you got locked up was because somebody checked you in at Central Prison." I was even more confused. I didn't know what that meant.

I wrote to Mark Katz relating this and a few days later I got a letter back. It began:

> I have to apologize. I'm the reason you are in segregation. I just realized this when you told me the explanation you were given. I have been posting excerpts from your songs and letters on your Facebook page and on two occasions I "checked in" to Central Prison. Since you have never used Facebook, this is probably confusing. To check in somewhere on Facebook is just to indicate that you were at a place. The reason I checked you in there was simply to indicate where you are. I thought it was an inconsequential thing—it's just a fact that you are in Central Prison. I have to say that I don't understand why this would get you in trouble. You don't have a computer or a phone so you didn't post anything yourself and you didn't instruct me to do anything. I wonder if the problem is that the Facebook posts might sound like you are somehow creating them from inside the prison.

Now I knew why exactly I was locked up, but it still smelled like bullshit to me. I mean, it's the most bogus of charges because it was Katz's computer that he made the posts with, and he's on the outside. I knew he was running my Facebook page and posting excerpts from my letters, but I didn't tell him what to post. He even sent me pictures of his Facebook screen with those posts that said, "Posted by Mark Katz." And these were class A offenses I was being charged with. They're the most serious kind and include holding hostages, rioting, assaulting a staff member, and escaping from prison.

Katz and other supporters of mine did everything they could to help me fight these charges. They consulted a lawyer, who agreed that the charges were bogus and said that many, many incarcerated people have social media pages. On advice from the lawyer, they wrote detailed letters to Central Prison's warden and to North Carolina's commissioner of prisons. Nothing I wrote or they wrote made a difference or even got a response. The charges were never dropped and for doing nothing I spent thirty-seven days in the hole.

Thirty-Seven Days in the Hole (Excerpt)

I've been nine years with no write-up, a model inmate
Maintain do the right thing and set the template
Salat prayed five a day, I fast Ramadan
No gambling, no drugs, resisting Shaitan
Good deeds and charity without a second thought
Done for the sake of Allah like the Prophet taught
Got no hate in my heart for another man
The things I want for myself, want for my brother man
Dream big, make plans and work hard
Got faith in myself and trust God
I can achieve and do something good for others
Maybe even free myself and my brothers
One day just outta the blue the blow was so cold

Handcuffed and then strip searched and threw me in the hole
No clue to what I had done or been accused of
A dam broke in my heart and a deluge of anger flooded my
    mind, how did I land here?
Right back in this hole where I did ten years
Sat back, studied my moves, what did I do wrong?
I know I didn't break no rules, just made a few songs
maybe I was getting' some buzz about to blow up
Internet showin' me love, I mean but so what?
I ain't did nothing deserving of persecution
I sat there scratching my head lost in confusion
COs come by, I speak they keep walkin'
Like they don't even see me or something or hear me talkin'
I realize they don't respect my being meek
When you try to be nice they start thinkin' something is sweet
So I had to raise my voice like Muthafucka Yo!
Who you think I am some kinda sucker hoe?!
Now they understand that speech so they turn around
Lock eyes and they see I ain't some kinda clown
They don't really want no smoke though I'm a Muslim
I'm six-one, three hundred and some change, a former
    hoodlum
The red flag security tag says that I'm violent
In other words not somebody to fuck around with
I don't like to act outside of my character
But back here all they respect is animals
So after I bark then they adjust
Now I ain't got to raise my voice or even cuss
Still though nobody don't know what I'm locked up fo'
Days start to turn into weeks I'm feelin' stuck yo
Can't talk to my mom on the telephone
Since I've been in the hole she feelin' so alone
My little sister died, Mama's babygirl
Life's so hard in that crazy world
And I can't help my mom or be a son for her
Give her a shoulder to cry on and comfort her
My wife wrote a letter said she needs me
I write back tryin' to be strong but it's not easy
Knowing that the people I love most are suffering

Every day I'm here strugglin'
But still got the support of my team
Released a few songs, getting' closer to my dreams
But in the hole dreams are turned to nightmares
Internal Affairs, after my sixteenth night here
Showed up at my door they said, "What up Rrome?"
I'd seen these guys before they heard my stuff on
SoundCloud maybe a few months back
They'd been curious to how I'd recorded the tracks
I told 'em back then that I did it on the telephone
They said they were feelin' my songs and liked Rrome Alone
Told me to keep it up it was fire
Which lifted my spirits and my confidence higher
Now they tellin' me something new about a write-up
Something 'bout a cellphone charge that they made light of
They said "Rrome we know you ain't got a phone
But the reason you're being charged is 'cause somebody's been
    posting on
Facebook and checked you in at CP"
I was confused 'cause I ain't even know what "checking in" was
    supposed to be
I asked them "Why y'all ain't tell me I was doing wrong
When you went on SoundCloud and heard my songs?"
They swore that SoundCloud was official
But it was the Facebook check-in that created the whole issue
I said, "Man, my sister Keisha made that profile
on Facebook I'm sure y'all knew about it the whole while
It's been at least two years since she made it
To get messages and keep people updated"
I told 'em I ain't never used a cellphone
And the internet wasn't around back when I was home
They told me I should put all that on a statement
I actually thought they were tryin' to help get all this
    straightened
So I obliged and wrote a statement up like they advised
They read it in my presence looked me in the eyes
Told me it was the best they'd ever read
Said I'd probably get the case dismissed which eased my head
See I wasn't just concerned about the State harassing me

But losing credit for being nine years infraction-free
That was part of the plan I had constructed
To go twenty-five years and not be interrupted
With bad conduct, get my sentence overturned
Do good deeds to try and show that I deserve
Another chance at freedom before the pearly gates
Maybe I could come home by 2038
The charge wasn't even really
A real charge but said my statement was confession and found
    me guilty
Give me thirty days in the hole
Took my canteen and visits for three months it left me swole
I told the chaplain it was baffling
She agreed, couldn't believe how everything unfolded and
    happened
And it hurt me to my soul that despite my innocence I did
    thirty-seven days in the hole!

The Alim Team

THE ONLY REASON I'M able to do what I'm doing is because I've been blessed with a team. This is really what separates me from others here on Death Row. There are people here that might be more talented than me, but they lack resources. The longer a person is incarcerated, the weaker his support system becomes, and on Death Row we are talking about guys who've been in prison for over twenty years. I want to highlight this fact so people on the outside will realize that there are others in here that are talented, too, and perhaps make resources available to them as has been done for me.

Over the past several years I've befriended several people who have made it possible for me to pursue my dreams of recording an album on Death Row and are helping me get the word out about the innocent people locked up here. This group—Tessie Castillo, Michael Betts II, Mark Katz, Nick Neutronz, and Wordsmith—have called themselves the Alim Team, and it's because of them that you can hear my music and read this book.

Although he is not part of the team, there would be no Alim Team if it weren't for Dr. Peter Kuhns, the former psychological program manager at Central Prison. In the early 2010s, he set up educational and therapy classes on Death Row that were taught by volunteers. Through that program I met Tessie Castillo, a writer who taught a journalism class at Central Prison in 2014. While she was volunteering at Central Prison, she wrote an editorial for the *News and Observer* about her experience. She said: "I don't see heartless killers, though they might have killed in a moment of heartlessness. I see anger problems, stubbornness, lack of self-control, immaturity, and miseducation. But in these men I also see pain, regret, a capacity for kindness and self-reflection—and a desire to be seen for what they are: flawed and very human." We maintained contact and she encouraged me to write. I was a contributor to two books that she edited, *Crimson Letters* and *Inside: Voices from Death Row*, that came out in 2020 and 2022.

Dr. Kuhns also brought in a group called Hidden Voices, led by Lynden Harris. I was selected by Dr. Kuhns to be one of six participants that worked with Hidden Voices to write a couple of plays, including one called *Serving Life*, which was later adapted for the stage and performed under the title *Count* by professional actors. In 2016, Lynden wanted us to record monologues for an art exhibition called *Serving Life: ReVisioning Justice*. That's how I met Michael Betts. He was a graduate student at Duke University at the time, but now he's a film studies professor at the University of North Carolina Wilmington. We work together closely and talk at least once a week. He's recorded hundreds of hours of me telling my story.

I'm gonna pause for a second to shout out Hidden Voices. Working with their team—Lynden Harris, Jennifer Thompson, Nancy Demorest, and Kathy Williams—was incredible, truly a once-in-a-lifetime opportunity for someone in my situation. We met every week for over two years—we talked and wrote, and it was a space to be open, vulnerable, and authentic. Lynden is a genius in her ability to draw stuff out of people. She guides so subtly. We didn't even know we were writing a play until she came in one day and handed us the script and was like, "This is what you guys have created." I read it, and it was 100 percent our words. But the way she structured it and made our individual contributions tell a larger story was amazing. This was *Serving Life*. We performed it for over a hundred people, both inmates and staff. People were laughing and crying, and afterward they came up and shook our hands and thanked us. After that I realized that, even though I was on Death Row, I could do meaningful things that could impact people on both sides of these walls.

While doing phone interviews with Tessie Castillo in 2020 to promote *Crimson Letters*, I spoke with a podcast host in Seattle named Dr. Darian Parker. When he learned that I rapped, he listened to my music on Sound-Cloud and introduced me to his brother Anthony "Wordsmith" Parker. Wordsmith is a rapper based in Baltimore who is also the founder and owner of the record label NU Revolution Entertainment. He's released some of my music on his label and has helped me promote my work through social media.

I've already talked about the other two members of the Alim Team, Mark Katz and Nick Neutronz. These five—Tessie, Mike, Mark, Nick, and Word—are my team. I never set out with the intention of forming an Alim Team. I didn't even know that I could assemble a team, or what its members would look like. None of this was a part of my plan. Allah brought them to me. And Alhamdulillah, He assembled an all-star cast. To top it off, they are good people, people with integrity and good character. I trust each of them unquestionably. It's not just luck that I got such a high-quality group of people, it's Allah. He says in the Qur'an:

> And whoever fears Allah and keeps his duty to Him, He will make a way for him to get out (from every difficulty). And He will provide him from (sources) he never could imagine. And whosoever puts his trust in Allah, then He will suffice him. Verily, Allah will accomplish his purpose.

Isn't that the truth? I put my trust in Him and He has sufficed me. Alhamdulillah!

Anger Is a Privilege That I Don't Have

A WHILE BACK, A MEMBER of my team connected me with a composer who was looking for someone to write a rap battle for a musical. I called him and he told me about the story and characters and said that the battle scene takes place in a prison. I was like, "Hell yeah!" I was ready to get to work. Then he let the cat out of the bag and said that the musical was gonna be on Broadway. When I got off the phone with him I couldn't contain my excitement. I called my mom and she said, "Jerome! You're gonna be on Broadway!" I said, "Inshallah!" She was crying, she was so excited. I called Jeannie and she said, "That is amazing, baby, I am so proud of you." I said, "Alhamdulillah!" In my mind I was doing karate chops, cartwheels, and somersaults. I wanted to celebrate. For me that meant buying myself an ice cream and then lying in bed and soaking it all in, letting myself imagine and dream.

I wrote some music for the composer, and he said he loved it, even called it extraordinary. But then he decided that he would only work with me under conditions that my team said were exploitative. They were really upset with this man and encouraged me to stop working with him. I understood their anger, but I felt that I had to take the opportunity regardless. I'm fortunate to have a team on the outside. I appreciate everything they do, and I appreciate their willingness to go to bat for me. It means a lot. But the way I felt about this was complicated, made even more so by the fact that people on my team were upset and trying to protect me from exploitation. I get it. But anger is a privilege that I don't have. I needed them to chew on that for a minute.

I'm not free. I'm like a slave. I don't get to talk back or express my displeasure. Any expression of discontent, physical or verbal, is a threat to security and order. A free person doesn't have to think about that. If somebody insults their dignity, then they are free to express their outrage. My dignity is insulted almost every day. When I interact with prison staff, I am never afforded the equality of a free person. I always feel like a suspect, like what I say isn't credible or trustworthy. So I learn to eat shit and keep on moving, even though every fiber in my being wants to explode. But I know the consequences. This is the life of the slave. Especially one with as many lashes on my back as I have.

Again, anger is not a privilege that I have.

So it's complicated when my friends are enraged when someone is exploiting me but I feel like I can't afford to let an opportunity pass me by. It's a moral tug-of-war. All I can do is hope they don't look down on me for eating shit. I eat it because I have to. Not because I love it. I've already done so much unpaid, uncredited work. But it doesn't deter me. I'm trying to dig out of a deep, deep pit that I dug for myself many years ago. I'm trying to do something that helps others, and I don't blink at the labor or sacrifice it requires. To be angry, to pass up opportunities that might feel demeaning, is selfish when I'm carrying others on my back. If I balked at everything that seems offensive, I'd never make any progress.

I realize that in the eyes of some opportunists, I'm a dumb nigga on Death Row. I hate to put it so crudely, but it's often how I feel treated and regarded. And that's what I'm trying to climb up out of. It's hard. It hurts sometimes, and it's a life of shit-eating. I never did end up working with that composer— he stopped answering my calls—but I don't have any regrets. I'm sure others will try to exploit me, but I ain't got time to feel sorry for myself. I'm too busy digging up.

The Zoom Solution

BY LATE 2020, I was still trying to figure out how we were gonna solve the technical problems we had been dealing with when recording my songs. And that's when I realized that Zoom was the solution. It took the coronavirus to bring it to my awareness, though. It's crazy, but if there had not been a pandemic, I still might not know about Zoom and therefore still wouldn't be able to record my rhymes in time to real music. When I was first recording, everything was just a cappella. I might have a beat in my head, but that didn't help me rhyme in a consistent tempo. So, let's say I recorded "White Cop." I wrote "White Cop" with the beat to KRS-One's "Black Cop" in my head. But when I recorded the a cappella over the phone to my own internal beat, I wasn't in the pocket—I was all over the place. I was unconsciously slowing down or speeding up, so it would be impossible to take my a cappella and lay it on the "Black Cop" instrumental. So that was my biggest hurdle: How was I gonna get my vocals recorded in perfect time to fit a beat?

For this to happen, I needed two things. I had to be able to hear the beat at the same time as I rapped, while the producer on the other end of the phone needed to be able to record my vocals without the beat. In a recording studio this wouldn't be a problem, but it was in my situation. The idea for a solution came one day when I was watching TV. I kept seeing stories about something called Zoom that people were using for online meetings. I started envisioning how it works. I pictured myself at home with a computer in a meeting with ten other people. I thought to myself, *If I'm on Zoom, wouldn't I be able to play a song that I have on my computer and let everybody in the meeting hear it?* It had to be possible. If so, then what if people were on their smartphones and not on the computer—wouldn't the same thing be possible? And if so, then couldn't I call someone on their smartphone and have them connect me to the meeting? Again, if that was possible, then I would be able to hear the same music that everybody else in the meeting could hear.

I thought about it some more. *Okay, if all these people are on the call and I'm sitting at home on my computer, shouldn't I be able to record everything in the meeting?* If I could record it, then what if I only wanted to record what was incoming to my computer and separate it from any output I was sending? Wouldn't that be possible? You know how you used to have to call the operator and get connected manually for a long-distance call? I just felt like there was something that connected the incoming with the outgoing and that they could therefore be separated by some type of cable or line. If Zoom worked like this, then my vocals could be recorded separate from the beat, even though the beat was playing in my ear. I mentioned this to Michael Betts, the audio engineer on the Alim Team, and he totally freaked out. He was like, "Dude, that's it! You figured it out! That's the solution right there!" I just smiled on my end on the phone because I've never used a computer or a cell phone and never been on the internet in my life. I was using outdated technology models that I vaguely understood and theorized that the principles had to be the same, just more developed with newer technology.

I was thrilled that we were able to find what we needed with Zoom, and if it wasn't for coronavirus, I may never have been exposed to it. Once we figured it out, Michael told Nick Neutronz about it, and we haven't looked back. The way Nick and I operate is like this: I usually call him at 9:30 a.m. on Tuesday, Thursday, and Saturday each week. He first logs in on his computer to open up a Zoom meeting, and then he uses his cell phone to call in to that meeting so the computer is the host and the cell phone is the other participant in the meeting. Once he enters the meeting on his cell phone, he merges my phone call in. Then he opens a recording session on his computer. This allows him to access whatever files he wants as well as the internet.

So, for instance, if he wants to play some of his tracks, he can just pull them up into the session on his computer and let them play. Because I'm on the Zoom call, I can hear whatever he plays through the phone, just like anyone else who was in the meeting. Sometimes he might pull up an instrumental from Spotify or YouTube and let it play. And sometimes I might have an idea for a beat that I'll sound out for him, and he'll play it on the keyboard, and we will create a track. We did this for the song "Raleigh OGs." I sounded out the melody and he played it on the synth and added a beat and a sample from the movie *Shaft*, and it was crazy. Sometimes I'll just listen to beats he's already made or beats that other producers have sent and select the ones I want to rap over. He'll play the track and I'll rap to it in time while he's recording it. I usually do at least two takes of the rhyme, just in case I messed up somewhere. Nick also likes to stack my vocals to compensate for the narrowness of the prison phone's sound.

Most of the time when we record there's a small delay, so the vocals aren't lined up right with the beat. However, because I rapped in time to the beat, and because my vocals and the beat are recorded on different tracks, he can fix it. Still, we had to learn how to communicate with each other about rhythm, and Nick had to get used to my style. Most of the time I don't start rapping on the first beat of the bar (which we call "the one") but on three or between beats three and four. When I first started working with Nick, I didn't know to describe beats using numbers, so I had a hard time explaining my approach. We might spend two or three fifteen-minute phone calls just trying to line up the vocals for a song. I would tell him things like, "Move the vocals forward just a hair," and he would be like, "Which way is forward?" Eventually we began to understand how the other was trying to communicate and it became a lot easier. After a while, Nick could line my vocal up with the beat without any direction from me.

Once he gets it lined up, he'll play it back to me, and I'm always amazed to hear myself rapping over a beat. Every single song sounds like a masterpiece to me. I'm so proud of what we've been able to accomplish. It's been really hard work, and most people have no idea the countless hours we've put into it to iron out all the wrinkles. A lot of people would've given up, so I'm truly grateful to have been working with Nick Neutronz. Me and that dude may not have reinvented the wheel, but we made it roll in a whole new way. And it shows in the quality of the sound. We're always looking to make it even better. For me, that's just another example of why what we are doing is so special. We are using technology in a way that hasn't been used before, and that's what's innovative.

Just think about it, the person who invented the phonograph never imagined it could be used as a musical instrument, but people in hip hop scratched records to make music. In the same way, the people who invented Zoom never imagined it would be used to record music over the phone from Death Row. Alhamdulillah!

A Major Milestone

ON JANUARY 30, 2021, I achieved a major milestone. I recorded a fifteen-minute video with Michael Betts. I can't describe how amped I was. I felt like I could finally exhale. For the most part, I've done just about everything that I can do to record and preserve my art, and now it's up to my people on the outside to shape it and mold it and get it seen and heard. Don't get me wrong, I'm gonna be involved in all of that too, but those are functions that can be performed without me. Now I've done it. It's unbelievable.

Three years earlier, I couldn't even imagine getting any video footage of me recorded. It just wasn't possible. In 2014 when I was working with Hidden Voices and they were coming inside the prison to talk and plan and work with us, we couldn't even get a tape recorder in to document our sessions. They wanted to bring cameras but weren't allowed. We wrote a play and performed it for over a hundred people but couldn't film it. So there's no

Cover art for the Rrome Alone song "If I'm a
Killer," by Cerron Hooks. Image of Alim Braxton
taken from a childhood photo.

recorded evidence that we even did it. When the warden allows the news media to film inside the prison, they can't show our faces. They aim the cameras at our feet. So how could I even imagine that one day I would be able to get recorded video footage of me rapping in here on Death Row? This is *huge*. But I had this vision, and I prayed to Allah to help me bring it to fruition. I believed in Him and Alhamdulillah, He has brought about the impossible. Just think about that. I didn't know how it was gonna work. In fact, if someone would've told me three years earlier that the sergeant would call me down to the multipurpose room and three COs were gonna sit a laptop in front of my face and allow me fifteen minutes to perform on camera, I would've said, "Yeah RIGHT"! But that's exactly what happened.

I had been practicing my rhymes for the last two days, trying to time myself to record six or seven songs in fifteen minutes. That morning I was nervous, but this was my shot, and I couldn't afford to choke just because I would be in a room with three COs. So when they called my name for the visit and I walked down the hall, I swear it felt like I was leaving the dressing room and making my way toward the stage in a packed arena. In my head I could hear all this crowd noise, people chanting my name. It's crazy because I had never experienced anything like that before, and I kept thinking that this is what it must be like moments before going onstage.

I stepped in the room and the COs got Michael Betts on screen. I had to wear my mask, so you couldn't see my mouth as I performed. But Michael said we could use that to our advantage and reuse the footage for multiple songs. Also, I was seated the whole time so it's not a full-body video, which is definitely limiting. But at least we've got *something*. Who else on Death Row has recorded songs and video footage to accompany it? That's something special, man. I was super proud of myself, and again I give All Praises to Allah! He is the All Powerful.

I've been holding onto this footage for now. I don't want it to leak out before we get to shape it like we want it. I want to keep adding to what we have before we start releasing, just in case they try and shut me down. I want the work to move forward even if I'm standing still. This time I'm prepared to suffer the consequences because I know what the rules are. Short-term loss for a long-term gain. If you aren't willing to sacrifice for what you believe in, then you don't really believe. And sometimes you might have to break a rule to advance a moral cause. Inshallah, if I can bring this vision into reality and open the doors for the innocent, then doing time in the hole and losing some of my privileges is a small price to pay for such a huge reward.

Jay-Z

ANYBODY WHO KNOWS ME knows that I consider Jay-Z to be the greatest rapper of all time. He is the ultimate example of success and the manifestation of everything I have wanted to be as an MC. The platinum records, sold-out venues, world tours, awards, and wealth as well as the respect of his peers and his impact on the culture. He's a philanthropist, a mentor to other rappers, a businessman, an icon of style and fashion, and a symbol of cool. He is connected to some of the most powerful people on earth and respected by people from all walks of life, whether they live on Death Row or in the White House.

That's the stuff I have dreamed about for myself. Seeing his success makes me think about what I might have accomplished had I been out there pursuing my own music career. Of course, while he was on a world stage for thirty years, I was in cell. All I could do was watch. But I'm glad I got to witness it. I got to see my dreams realized, even if I'm not the one living the dream. That lets me know that it was possible. So I love Jay-Z.

I've learned a lot about rapping by studying his rhymes. One time, Cmurf and I did a version of Jay-Z and Eminem's song "Renegade," where I filled in for Jay-Z and he took Em's spot. I followed Jay-Z's distinct pattern, using the same number of syllables and rhymes but replacing all the words. It was like a combination of a crossword and a fill-in-the-blank puzzle. For instance, Jay-Z said, "I had to hustle, my back to the wall, ashy knuckles." Counting the syllables between each comma you have five syllables, then five more, then four. I replaced his words with, "I had no knowledge, a little book sense, bagged 'fore college." Notice I also followed his rhyme scheme: he said, "had to hustle . . . ashy knuckles" and I said, "had no knowledge . . . bagged 'fore college." I can't tell you how fun this was. But I would only do this with an artist I greatly admire. I'm not gonna spend too much time imitating just anybody's rhyme scheme—I'd rather create my own. But Jay-Z is a master, so it was like learning from a sage. If I was teaching somebody how to rap, that is the method I would employ.

Well, I can never accomplish everything that Jay-Z has accomplished. But I still have a dream. I envision my music making its way to his ears, and after hearing it, he not only likes it but wants to work with me! That would be the ultimate validation. Nobody else might know what to do with me as an artist behind these walls, but I believe if Jay-Z hears me, he'll know. That's the dream!

The Best Human Being I've Ever Met

THERE IS NO WAY I can end this book without some more Jeannie. We men often write our women out of history, so I need to say that Jeannie is truly the hero of my story. I've already talked about how we met in high school and then reunited twenty-seven years later. But I want to say more about her character. The more I learn about this woman, the more I admire her. Her resilience is unparalleled. I mean it with the fullness of my heart when I say that Jeannie is truly the best human being I've ever met. (Of course, my mother is in a special category where there are no equals.)

I worry about my wife. She's a double amputee (she had a second amputation in 2020) and has diabetes, high blood pressure, kidney failure, congestive heart failure, and several other ailments associated with these diseases. She'll need dialysis for the rest of her life and depends on a transportation service with a specially equipped van that can handle her motorized wheelchair. Sometimes the van doesn't show up. Many times, she's had to check in to the hospital for days at a time. And she takes care of three kids all by herself.

Jeannie is a very proud woman and doesn't ask anyone for help or want anyone's pity. But I mention these hardships because I want people to know what kind of person she is. Prophet Muhammad, peace be upon him, says that a man may marry a woman for four things: her religion, her wealth, her beauty, or her lineage. He says that the best woman to marry is the religious one. That's a loose translation. But he's saying that it's best to marry a woman based on her morals and good conduct and character. And I immediately found this to be true about Jeannie. She has a beautiful personality and good character and unlike physical beauty, these qualities will never fade. But don't get me wrong—she is *fine*!

Jeannie is one of the most selfless people I know. Sometimes I only learn about her sacrifices by accident. One time my nephew told me he was selling a queen size bedroom set and asked if I knew anyone who might be interested. Jeannie immediately came to mind. When I called her house her oldest son answered, so I asked about everyone's sleeping arrangements. He told me that he and his sister each had a twin-size mattress and his younger brother slept in the hospital bed that had been sent to the house for Jeannie. I asked him, "Well, where does Jeannie sleep?" And he said, "Mom sleeps on the couch."

I felt my heart drop! Jeannie and I had been together over three years and never had she mentioned that she slept on the couch. I felt so much love and admiration for her in that moment because I realized that she had willingly sacrificed her own comfort for the sake of her kids. And she did it without any desire for recognition! She was in the hospital at the time, so I called her there and asked her how come she'd never told me that she slept on the couch all this time. She just said she wanted her kids to have their own beds. I told her about the queen size bedroom set and said that I was going to get it for her. And with some help I did—Alhamdulillah! When we got everything set up, she gushed with joy and pride for like a week straight! May Allah continue to bless us.

I do everything I can for Jeannie, but I know my situation is not easy on her. It was especially hard when I was on lock-up for thirty-seven days in 2020. She's accustomed to talking to me on the phone every day, but I was deprived of my phone and visitation privileges. When I was finally able to talk to Jeannie, I really got a chance to hear how all this affected her. She said she was afraid. Afraid that the system will keep me from being able to

Jeannie Bunch, Raleigh,
North Carolina, August 13,
2021. Photo by Mark Katz.

see her or talk to her. But she's also afraid that I will choose my music over her. I understood. It's been hard on her, and this is the part about prison that the "lock 'em up and throw away the key" advocates don't understand or care about.

You can't really understand unless you have a loved one in prison. Imprisonment punishes the people who love you just as much as it punishes you. When they throw me in the hole, they are throwing my mom in the hole, they are throwing my wife in the hole. When they punish me, they punish them. I told Jeannie that I wasn't choosing my music over her. All this is for her, it's for my mom, it's for all my family. It's for Sabur and the other innocent people on Death Row. I told her that with this music I can get attention. People can become aware of what I am doing. They can become aware of Sabur. How can I generate support if I don't speak? And the more support I have the harder it is to treat *me* unjustly. She said she felt better after that and told me she believed. Then I spit a rap I wrote for her and that made her smile. She told me I needed to record that one! I'll say it again: she is the best human being I've ever met.

Sometimes when I'm talking to Jeannie, I ask her to dream with me and tell me what she wants. She always insists that she is fine and just having me is enough. But I want her to dream. One of her biggest needs is transportation, so I once asked her what kind of car she would want. Being modest, she said it didn't matter. "But if you had your pick of any vehicle, what would it be?" "Well," she said, "maybe a Jeep Grand Cherokee." I said, "Of all the cars in the world you'd rather have a Jeep Grand Cherokee than a BMW, a Ferrari, or a Maybach?!" "Okay," she admitted, "well, maybe a Range Rover." I said, "All right then. Now you're giving me something to work toward. Inshallah, one day I'm gonna get you a Range Rover. And when I do, I'm gonna make it wheelchair accessible and get you a pair of them Gucci shades—that way you can look down on the haters and smile as you pull off!" She liked that! A thousand times since then I've told her I'm gonna get her that Range Rover, and she just says, "I know you are, baby."

When I married Jeannie, I knew that Allah had rewarded me with a jewel. But because of her health, I also knew that she may not live very long. We may have another three years together, or five, or ten, or twenty. Allah knows best. But I know in my heart and mind that however long Allah intends to let her live, I will give her the very best that I can give.

It Was a Good Day

'VE HAD ONE HELL OF A JOURNEY, long and full of obstacles. When I think back to 2020, it's hard to imagine how much happened in just that year. It seemed like I could hardly get a break. My sister Keisha died in February. A friend of mine, Billy, died in March. Coronavirus came and shut down the country. I wasn't able to see my mom or Jeannie or anyone in person for most of the year. Ahmaud Arbery was murdered in February. Breonna Taylor was murdered in March. Then in May the world watched a cop kneel on the neck of George Floyd for almost nine minutes. Protests erupted all throughout the country that summer, and even around the world. I went to the hole for thirty-seven days for some bullshit. Lost my privileges for three months, got stripped of my imam position. Jeannie lost her other leg. Dude got stabbed just a few feet from me and nobody blinked. At the end of the year, I was like, *Man, please just let me go home, I've been through enough!*

Alhamdulillah, 2021 was a better year. I recorded a few dozen tracks, released several singles, and even worked with my team to create a video for my song, "Live on Death Row." I was able to record a video of myself for the first time in my life, and I developed a way to record my songs through Zoom. I started the process of writing this book. The local CBS station aired a story about me. I stayed busy. Often, when I accomplish something, I don't take the time to enjoy it because I'm like, "Alhamdulillah, now what's next?" I'm still working on the dream, but let me mark one more moment and share one last story.

On September 20, 2021, WKNC 88.1 FM played a forty-five-minute interview with me by DJ Whippopotamus. Plus, they played my new song, "Live on Death Row," and I was able to hear it clearly for the first time. It was amazing! I was so impressed with the production. Nick did a really good job, and after hearing it, I had no more concerns about the sound quality of my vocals. All along my biggest fear was that my vocals would sound like I was recording with a two-dollar Fisher Price toy microphone. But those worries were no more. The vocals on "Live on Death Row" sounded studio quality to me. If I hadn't recorded them over the phone myself, I would've never known.

It was crazy hearing myself talk for forty-five straight minutes. I can't believe they aired the entire interview—I had never heard anything like that before on WKNC. I only told a handful of people about it before it aired. I didn't want to announce it like on a bullhorn or nothing because I didn't want to portray it like it was a big deal. I mean, it was a big deal for me, but you can never gauge how people might receive something. Still, word spread quickly. I was at Sabur's cell when it came on and I told him I was gonna bounce because I wanted to go to my cell and listen with no distractions. As I stepped into the dayroom, I saw several people nodding at me and pointing to their radio. Some of them were sharing earphones with others. I heard people saying, "Go to 88.1, Bank is on the radio!" (Bank is one of my nicknames on the Row.) I nodded at everybody and threw up my fist as a salute for showing support, and I went to my cell and listened to the whole interview. It was the first time getting to hear how I sound, my accent, my use of slang, and just my flow of speech.

After it was over, I performed salat and then it was lock-in time for count. During count I tuned in to 88.1 because they have a local hip hop segment, and they played "Live on Death Row" again! I was so amped. It was the second time that day that they played my song and the third time it's been on the radio. Even if it's never played again, even if I never release my album, I can always say that my song was played three times on the radio. I was so happy I can't even put it into words.

After count, I called my mom. She told me she listened to my entire interview in her car. She texted my brother Chris to make sure he was listening, too. He was at work, but he tuned in. She told him that she was so proud of me, that even on Death Row I was living my dream. She started crying telling me about it, and she said Chris got emotional, too. Ain't nobody a bigger fan of Rrome Alone than Chris Braxton. Anytime I call him and he's in his car, he's listening to one of my songs on his sound system. My mom has told me on more than one occasion that Chris says that I am the Greatest Rapper Ever! It felt good hearing my mom say she was proud of me. She had a hundred compliments to fill my heart. She said she loved the interview, and that it was just amazing to sit in her car and listen to her son talking *on the radio*. I was smiling so hard my cheeks had to be touching my ears.

While I was on the phone, a guy from another block came by the window and threw his fist up at me and pounded his chest while nodding his head in the affirmative to signify his approval. I nodded back and threw up my fist. When I finished, my friend Chubb came over and we went to my cell. He told me how impressed he was and then pulled a piece of paper out of his pocket and started looking around for a pen. I thought he wanted to write something down, but he said, "Let me get your autograph, bruh." We both started laughing and then he told me I did my thang. "That was a good interview," he said. "I told you they was gonna have your ass on the radio, and I liked everything you said." Then we dapped it up and hugged. He asked if had I talked to Sabur yet. I told him not yet. He said, "I can't wait to hear his reaction, he probably over there crying right now with his soft ass!" We laughed, and then I bounced to go to Sabur's block.

As I stepped in Big Ray gave me a fist bump and said, "Good job." He's another guy on the Row with an innocence claim. He's in his sixties and is a huge musclebound guy and former body builder. As I passed him, a guy named Al told me he heard my song and thought it was good. I thanked him and headed upstairs. When I got up top, Carl said, "I just heard some dude on the radio named Bank and he said he wanted 150 mil for his record contract so he can get his homeboy who's got cancer off the Row." I smiled at him. Carl had been diagnosed with cancer about four or five months before. He said, "Then he started talkin' about some motherfucker named Stacey Tyler!" I chuckled and moved on. Next a guy named Rabbit stuck his head out and said, "I heard you on the radio. Great job." "I appreciate it," I said, and went to Sabur's cell. As soon as I stepped in, we dapped up with a loud clap and hugged. Then he smiled and started nodding his head up and down and said, "You did your thang. I was impressed. That was a damn good interview." Then I sat down and we just rehashed everything that was said.

While we were talking, my man Salih came over and told me that he heard the whole interview. What impressed him the most was that I didn't make it just about me—I represented the Row. He said, "You talked about us and I just wanted to tell you I appreciate it because you represented me well." Then he told me his sister wanted to hook up with me. We laughed.

After Salih left, I asked Sabur how it felt hearing his name on the radio, how it felt to hear me proclaim his innocence. "Honestly, it felt good," he said. "You know, everybody always see you up in my cell and they know that something is going on but they just don't know what it is. They probably be thinkin', 'What Alim see in this motherfucker?' They know you workin' on this music but they don't know what my part is." I said, "Now they know." He nodded. "Now they know, and truthfully I wouldn't want it coming from anybody but you." I soaked that in for a minute and then I asked him what he meant. "It means more coming from you," he said. "If it was my lawyers, they get paid to say that shit. And my family, that's what they supposed to say. But coming from you it means more because you are my best friend." I smiled at him 'cause I knew he was getting emotional and I was, too. We finally dapped up and he said, "I love you, bruh." I told him, "I love you too, akh."

Sabur and I exchanged salaams and then I went to another pod for a minute. Nadim gave me the thumbs up and so did Big Dog and Pitbull. Kazim told me, "You know I ain't never listened to no interview for that long, but I listened to the whole thang." I told him I appreciated it. Then I stopped to holler at Cmurf. He said he heard the whole interview and was feeling everything I said. The only thing he didn't like is when the dude asked if there were other rappers on Death Row. He thought I was gonna mention him, B-Dot, and Money Ray, but I just said that there were others without mentioning names. I told him I didn't want to risk leaving somebody out. If I named him, B-Dot, and Money Ray there are others who might've felt snubbed. He understood. I bounced and then came back to my pod to call Jeannie. She didn't get a chance to hear it live because she was in the hospital, so she went to the WKNC website and listened to it later. She told me how proud she was. That night B-Dot came over to my cell to show me a hook he was working on. He said what I was doing was inspiration and motivation for him. He encouraged me to keep doing what I was doing. I felt that to the heart.

Alhamdulillah, it was a good day.